Praise for
THE ESSENTIAL ZOHAR

"In elegant prose, Rav Berg takes a complex
subject and renders it accessible in this
presentation of a venerable Jewish study.
Word by word, passage by passage, he unravels
apparent and transcendent meanings in these
parables of the human condition, exemplified in
biblical lore. Berg beautifully references the
significance of these teachings today,
acknowledging the inherent difficulty of
spiritual development while also highlighting
its rewards."

—*NAPRA ReView*

"Insightful . . . Berg writes accessibly about
the Zohar as a way people can tap into cosmic
energies that are available for personal and
universal salvation."

—*Publishers Weekly*

Also by RAV P. S. BERG

Wheels of a Soul

Time Zones

To the Power of One

Miracles, Mysteries & Prayer (two volumes)

Secret Codes of the Universe

Immortality

Education of a Kabbalist

Kabbalistic Astrology

The Essential
ZOHAR

THE SOURCE OF
KABBALISTIC WISDOM

RAV P. S. BERG

Bell Tower · New York

Published by Bell Tower, New York, New York.
Member of the Crown Publishing Group, a division of Random House, Inc.
www.crownpublishing.com

Originally published in hardcover by Bell Tower in 2002.

Bell Tower and colophon are registered trademarks of Random House, Inc.

Printed in the United States of America

Design by Fearn Cutler de Vicq

Library of Congress Cataloging-in-Publication Data
Berg, Philip S.
The essential Zohar : the source of kabbalistic wisdom / by P. S. Berg.
Includes bibliographical references.
1. Zohar.   2. Cabala.   3. Bible.   O.T. Pentateuch—Commentaries.   I. Title.
BM525.A59 B47   2002
296.1'62—dc21   2001039565

ISBN 0-609-80731-5

10 9 8 7 6 5 4 3

FIRST PAPERBACK EDITION 2004

For my wife, Karen.
In the vastness of cosmic space and the infinity of lifetimes, it is my
bliss to be your soul mate and to share a lifetime with you.

CONTENTS

The Essential Zohar

Part One

FOUNDATIONS

THE ZOHAR AND KABBALAH

The Zohar is the central text of Kabbalah, and Kabbalah is the spiritual heritage of all humankind. Though it is often defined as the mystical tradition of Judaism, Kabbalah predates and transcends identification with any religion, nation, or ethnicity. Kabbalah is a body of spiritual wisdom and teachings, but it is not "religious," as that word is often understood. Kabbalah is not about rote obedience of laws or commandments. It is not based on literal interpretation of scriptures, nor does it include fear of punishment as a motivation for observance. Moreover, unlike traditions that celebrate ecstatic or transcendent approaches to divine wisdom, Kabbalah includes logical analysis of spiritual matters as an important tool. As in quantum physics or genetics, however, logic in Kabbalah can take challenging and paradoxical forms. To fully grasp the kabbalistic principles as they are presented in the Zohar, it is best to discard both conventional religious expectations and linear, mechanistic styles of rational thought. Science tells us that an electron can exist in two places at once, even at opposite ends of the universe. Kabbalah does not ask us to accept anything more radical than that—or anything less radical, either!

It is most useful to think of Kabbalah in terms of tools, practical applications, guidebooks, and sometimes delphic utterances, rather than as religion or academic philosophy. By doing so, we can begin to put these tools to work in our own lives. We can also eliminate preconceptions that are utterly foreign to the true teachings of the sages. Kabbalah and the Zohar belong to everyone who has a sincere desire to learn, grow, and transform.

When the Creator brought the world into being, it was not His intention to include the pain and suffering that today beset us. Kabbalah, in common with other spiritual traditions, teaches that the negativity that afflicts humankind came about through the temptation and fall of primordial man. The kabbalists have used the word *chaos* to describe the negative circumstances that surround us—the "Murphy's Law" environment in which things will go wrong if they possibly can. Chaos is indeed an apt word. It is the opposite of harmony with the Creator, or more precisely, the unity with Him that once existed and will one day be regained.

Achieving this unity, according to Kabbalah, is the true purpose of lives: to restore Creation to the state that God intended for it, and to reenter the Eden from which we were exiled by Adam's sin. To make possible this return to paradise, the Creator has provided us with powerful spiritual tools, including the Sabbath, the Hebrew language and alphabet, and many others. Most of these tools are identified with Judaism in the public mind. But they, like the redemption they are intended to foster, are the birthright of everyone. Making this clear is an important purpose of this book, and of Kabbalah as a whole.

The Zohar is a very long book—a complete translation comprises many volumes—but even at full length the sages of Kabbalah view it as a concentrated distillation of infinite wisdom. To the kabbalists, the Zohar is more like a finely polished gem than an object made of paper and ink. Like a diamond or ruby, the Zohar is hard and durable. It is ageless. It shines as brightly today as it did at the time of its creation. Again, like a jewel, it is easily hidden, and there have been centuries in which its very existence was known to only a few.

Moreover, the Zohar has many facets and colors, depending on the angle and the spiritual light in which it is viewed. Perhaps it is no surprise that one of history's greatest kabbalists, Rabbi Moses Chaim Luzzatto (1707–1746) was a diamond merchant in Amsterdam.

Among secular scholars and historians there is controversy surrounding the authorship and chronology of the tradition's most important texts, but the kabbalists themselves are very clear on these points. The first book of Kabbalah, the *Sefer Yetzirah* (*The Book of Formation*) was revealed by the Creator to Abraham the Patriarch. Since this occurred four hundred years before the revelation of the Ten Utterances (or Commandments), the *Sefer Yetzirah* preceded the written Bible by many centuries. In fewer words than a slender paperback, the *Sefer Yetzirah* describes how Creation was accomplished through the distinct energies of the twenty-two letters of the Hebrew alphabet and the letters' numerological significance. The teachings of the *Sefer Yetzirah*, however, are so compressed as to be impenetrable to all but very elevated souls. If the Zohar is like a shining, multifaceted jewel, the *Sefer Yetzirah* is a small but perfectly cut diamond whose proportions can be appreciated only by a highly trained eye.

The Authorship and Structure of the Zohar

It was in the second century C.E., during the Roman occupation of what is now Israel, that the Zohar was revealed by the Creator to Rabbi Shimon bar Yochai and his son Elazar, who had taken refuge from the Romans in a mountain cave. This is a very firm kabbalistic teaching, although the origin of the Zohar is a subject of debate among academics. Many scholars maintain that the Zohar was written by the eleventh-century kabbalist Moses de Leon or by others among his contemporaries. When the Zohar is truly understood, however, it becomes clear that only Rabbi Shimon could have composed the work.

When the historians elect Moses de Leon as the author of the Zohar, they ignore the opinion of such great kabbalists as Moses Cordovero, Shlomo Alkabetz, Joseph Caro, Isaac Luria, Moses Luzzatto, and many others—men for whom the Zohar was a way of life, rather than a field of study, and who were unanimous in their agreement that Rabbi Shimon was the author of the Zohar. The underlying assumptions of these great men were that the man who wrote the Zohar must have been on the same level of spirituality as its contents, and that only Rabbi Shimon fit that description.

In the seclusion of the cave, Rabbi Shimon was visited twice a day by the prophet Elijah, who revealed to him the contents of the Zohar. The text comprises a commentary on the Bible and contains several sections. The main section, which bears the general title of *Sefer haZohar,* is generally connected and related to the weekly portion of the Torah. To this are attached: (1) *Idra Rabbah* (The Greater Assembly), which was actually written when Rabbi Shimon and his son Elazar emerged from the cave and selected eight disciples; these eight, together with Rabbi Shimon and his son, formed the "The Great Assembly" where, for the first time, the esoteric, internal teachings of the Torah were revealed; (2) *Sifra diTzenuta* (The Book of the Veiled Mystery) deals with the structure of the creative process; (3) *Sitrei Torah* (Secrets of the Torah) treats the power of the divine Names and how they are used to access the immense power of the cosmos; (4) *Idra Zuta* (The Lesser Assembly) describes those teachings of Rabbi Shimon bar Yochai that were not revealed during the Greater Assembly, but only on the day of Rabbi Shimon's death; (5) *Ra'aya Mehemna* (The Faithful Shepherd), Moses, deals with those cosmic precepts and doctrines not covered in the discourses between Elijah the Prophet and Rabbi Shimon bar Yochai; (6) *Midrash haNe'elam* (The Recondite Exposition) contains a vast collection of scriptural exposition concerning the method of numerology, that is, the permutations and

combinations of the letters of the *Aleph Beth* and the Hebrew nu-
merals; (7) *Zohar Hadash* (The New Zohar) is an independent commentary along the same lines as the Zohar, but it embraces, in
addition to the Torah, the Five *Megillot* (Scrolls): The Song of
Songs, Ruth, Lamentations, Ecclesiastes, and Esther; (8) *Tikunei
Zohar* (Emendations of the Zohar) addresses the same general subject matter as the Zohar but also discourses on teachings that are
specifically directed to the Age of Aquarius; (9) *Tosefta* (Additions)
adds some fragmentary supplements to the Zohar in which references to the *Sefirot* are made.

One should not take this to mean that the secrets of the Zohar
were revealed only to Rabbi Shimon. His teacher, Rabbi Akiva, and
several others before him were fully versed in all the teachings of
the Zohar. In fact, the entire understanding of Kabbalah was presented in its oral form to Israel on Mount Sinai. Many understood
the dazzling truths of Jewish mysticism, but few could make others
see and understand them. For this, the written text of the Zohar, we
would have to wait for Rabbi Shimon.

Why was Rabbi Shimon chosen to set down the teachings of
the Zohar in preference to his teacher, Rabbi Akiva, or indeed any
of the other giants of Kabbalah who preceded him? This problem
has been the source of many commentaries and parables; it is often
stressed, for instance, that through his fugitive and solitary life,
Rabbi Shimon was able to overcome the physical restraints and
limitations that normally prevent the attainment of higher levels of
spiritual consciousness. He was thus able to transcend the laws governing time and space, thereby acquiring root knowledge of all existence as we experience it on this earthly plane.

The first text of the Zohar was in Aramaic, the vernacular of
the region at that time. As with the *Sefer Yetzirah*, however, the wisdom of the Zohar was out of harmony with the consciousness of its
time—nor was this disharmony limited to the realm of the intel-

lect. Kabbalah teaches that the Zohar is an energy source in a very physical sense. Contemporary writers on Kabbalah compare the Zohar to an overwhelmingly powerful source of electrical power: Until the world was ready to make use of electricity, the presence of such a power source would be useless, and perhaps even dangerous. Therefore the Zohar was hidden away for more than ten centuries; Rabbi Shimon himself predicted that the concealment would last twelve hundred years.

The Dissemination of Kabbalah

During the thirteenth century, the Zohar came into the possession of the Spanish kabbalist Rabbi Moses de Leon. How this took place is not completely clear, as is true of most things that occurred more than seven hundred years ago. According to kabbalistic tradition, Rabbi de Leon discovered the text in the very cave where it had been concealed by Rabbi Shimon during the Roman persecution. This much is certain: After Rabbi de Leon transcribed the Zohar in 1279, Spain soon became the center of the study and practice of Kabbalah, and incomplete translations of the Zohar began to appear there over the next two hundred years.

Rabbi Isaac Luria (1534–1572) inaugurated what is today seen as the Golden Age of kabbalistic study and practice. While still a teenager living with his family in Cairo, Rabbi Luria was introduced to the Zohar. He then began a period of intense concentration and meditation on the sacred text, which included mystical revelations of Rabbi Shimon, his son Rabbi Elazar, and the great sage and martyr Rabbi Akiva. At the behest of his farsighted instructors, Rabbi Luria left Cairo for the village of Safed, in Galilee, where a kabbalistic community was flourishing under the leadership of Rabbi Moses Cordovero. Rabbi Luria spent the remainder of his short life in Safed. There he lived as a visionary scholar whose insights on the Zohar systematized and explained the text's fundamental concepts. Like a number of history's great philosophical minds, Rabbi Luria never wrote a word. His teachings were transcribed by his disciple Rabbi Chaim Vital.

Rabbi Luria died in 1572. Rabbi Vital survived him by almost forty years, though his transcriptions of Rabbi Luria's teachings were never disclosed during his lifetime. Indeed, it was Vital's wish that they never be revealed. When they were eventually revealed, however, a key step was taken toward bringing Kabbalah to all humanity, a process that continues to this day.

In the sixteenth century, Rabbi Abraham Azulai wrote the following in the preface to his treatise, *The Light of the Sun:* "From the year 1540 and onward the basic levels of Kabbalah must be taught publicly to everyone young and old. Only through Kabbalah will we forever eliminate war, destruction and man's inhumanity to his fellow man." The Zohar itself states that in succeeding generations even young children will understand Kabbalah and the inner truths of our world. And now the time has come to introduce the Zohar to the world at large in a way that is spiritually enlightening, intellectually accessible, and true to the spirit of the work as a whole.

Issues of composition and authorship of the book are relevant, but they must be understood in the context of the single most important fact about the Zohar: *It is a holy book.* Every word of it is sacred, every letter is a connection with the divine. Kabbalists throughout the centuries have described the Zohar in rhapsodic terms. There were even times when Kabbalah's veneration of the Zohar was criticized as a version of idol worship, but this is a shortsighted misunderstanding. In literary terms, the Zohar is like the shield of Achilles in the *Iliad.* It contains and expresses all of life. In scientific terminology, the Zohar is like a holographic image of creation. Everything is in it, if we know how to look closely enough. By venerating the Zohar, we pay homage to all of God's work.

The power of spiritual literature is difficult to define, but we recognize it intuitively. There is a sense that this is the truth, not so much historically as emotionally and spiritually. This, after all, is the real essence of kabbalistic truth. It is the reason that Kabbalah teaches that our world is the center of the universe—not physically, but spiritually.

As a reading experience, this book of selections aspires to be more than the sum of its parts. As you progress, you will notice three distinct but interwoven elements. First, the Zohar is a commentary on the Bible, including its narratives, characters, laws, descriptive passages, and even the genealogies. Second, it is a highly detailed map of the spiritual landscape that has come into being since the creation of the universe—or even before that creation—and that is still in the process of coming into being at this very moment. Finally, the Zohar is a set of practical instructions and tools for successfully traveling that well-defined yet ever-changing spiritual landscape, and ultimately attaining the transformation that is the true purpose of our lives.

Finding these instructions involves a certain amount of reading between the lines, but doing so is absolutely essential to the true experience of Kabbalah. We must not only think about these teachings, and feel them in our hearts, we must put them into practice. When you reach the end of the book, you will have learned much more Kabbalah than is explicitly indicated by the table of contents. But "learn" does not really describe the intention of the Zohar, or of Kabbalah itself. Implicitly or explicitly, the kabbalistic teachings are a call to action. The goal of the book is for readers to gain not only timeless wisdom but also practical applications that will benefit them, all humanity, and even, according to kabbalistic teachings, the inhabitants of the Upper Worlds. Although the Zohar may seem abstract, obscure, and even intimidating, at its foundation it is a very practical philosophy of life that intends to change and improve our experience of the world as we encounter it every day. The teachings of the Zohar concern not only the collective experience of humanity but also the stories of individual human beings—parents and children, students and teachers, friends and antagonists. "As above, so below" is a tenet of Kabbalah. Though the Zohar's stories were written thousands of years ago and concern the spiritual macrocosm, *your* story is within them. The meaning of *your* life and the means to *your* spiritual growth and transformation are contained in these teachings. The purpose of this book, and the purpose of my life's work, is to help you to discover them, recognize them, and take action in accordance with what you have learned.

Consider this analogy. When we are first becoming acquainted with another person, recognition of that person is based on physical appearance. Lacking any experience with the thoughts and feelings of the new acquaintance, we have no firmly grounded expectations. We may have hopes and fears concerning the new person who has come into our lives, but we do not yet have *trust*.

As time passes and the relationship grows, we begin to know our new friend's mind and heart. We begin to "see" this person with our spiritual eyes as well as our physical senses. This may take place over a period of years. We may see our friend every day, or perhaps only less frequently, but once the relationship has passed a certain point face-to-face contact becomes less important. Long separations may take place with no effect on the relationship. We may miss seeing our friend, but this is really the absence of a *physical* experience, because in truth we are deprived only at the level of our physical senses. The emotional and spiritual bond that has formed is not affected by absence, because it exists beyond the dimension of physical experience. Our friend's mind and heart remains interwoven with our own, unchanged.

In fact, when people have really gotten to know one another very well, whole conversations can take place entirely within their heads. We know what our friend would say if he or she were present, and we can literally "hear" it being said in our thoughts. This kind of internal dialog can continue in a relationship for a very long time. And finally, when the separation ends, the friendship is intact and is quickly able to resume.

This same paradigm can and should exist in our relationship with the Creator. Our purpose in life is first to recognize God, then to understand His presence in our lives, and ultimately to achieve unity with His nature. This is a continuing process. For most people, or for most souls, it requires many lifetimes for completion. But once we have genuinely achieved a first step, we quite naturally go forward. Once we have internalized the reality of the Creator's love and have learned to recognize His Light in the workings of our everyday lives, we are well on the way toward the unity with God that is our true purpose.

This is not primarily an intellectual process. If it were, we could be "talked out of it." But once you have learned how to walk, no one can convince you that it is not possible. No one forgets how to swim or how to ride a bicycle; Kabbalah and the Zohar exist to help you gain comparable abilities in the spiritual dimension of your life. They are tools for use in the completion of a very large and important project, which is the transformation of your being from what it is now to what the Creator wants and intends for you or—as the kabbalists express it—from a being of self-serving desire into one of desire for the purpose of sharing with others.

This is not a scholarly book, nor does it aim to be one. It is, however, congruent with the true nature of the Zohar in ways that elude academic or historical scholarship. Much of the Zohar is about friends traveling and talking together—sometimes meeting new people or seeing unusual sights, but often just sharing their questions and insights. In *The Essential Zohar*, I invite you to take a walk with me along the scenic pathways of this sacred book. We will not see everything the Zohar has to offer; indeed, that could take a lifetime. Instead, we will visit selected places in the text and focus our attention on understanding them, both on their own terms and in the context of the contemporary world.

All the selections in this volume are, I believe, *essential*, but not all are essential in the same way. Some have been chosen because they are representative of the Zohar as a whole. Over the course of the Zohar's many volumes, virtually all of the major episodes of the biblical narrative are discussed and interpreted. The interpretations are all strikingly original and spiritually enlightening, but collectively they compose a category that could be called biblical exegesis.

Other selections in this volume are distinguished more by their differences than by their shared characteristics. Their form is usually that of a dialog between friends, but the actual events of the episodes may vary a great deal. Sometimes nothing out of the ordinary happens. In other cases, people disappear into thin air, or narrowly escape injury. There is always the flash of insight into a higher reality, however, that in literary terms would be called an epiphany. These sections are really the essence of *The Essential Zohar*. Although it is by no means true that they offer more important spiritual teachings than the explicitly biblical sections, they are a different category of reading experience. They offer wisdom and insight, and there is a level of humor that is very different from what we might expect from a deeply spiritual book.

The Zohar and the Hebrew Alphabet

Suffice it to say, the Zohar is full of surprises. For more than two thousand years, the Zohar has transformed the lives of its students. Daily perusal of the text, even without any attempt at translation or "understanding" fills our consciousness with the Light. Even scanning of the Zohar by those unfamiliar with the Hebrew alphabet accomplishes the same result. Consider the passage below:

1. בְּרֵישׁ הוּרְמָנוּתָא דְמַלְכָּא, גָּלִיף גְּלוּפֵי בִּטְהִירוּ עִלָּאָה בּוּצִינָא דְּקַרְדִינוּתָא, וְנָפֵיק גּוֹ סְתִים דִּסְתִימוּ מֵרָזָ״א דְּאֵי״ן סוֹ״ף, קוּטְרָא בְּגוּלְמָא נָעִיץ בְּעִזְקָא לָא חִוָּור וְלָא אוּכַם וְלָא סוּמָק וְלָא יָרוֹק, וְלָא גָוָון כְּלָל. כַּד מָדֵיד מְשִׁיחָא, עָבֵיד גּוֹוְנִין לְאַנְהָרָא לְגוֹ. בְּגוֹ בּוּצִינָא, נָפֵיק חַד נְבִיעוּ, דִּמְנֵּיהּ אִצְטַבְּעוּ גּוֹוְנִין לְתַתָּא.

The letters themselves, even if we do not consciously know Hebrew or Aramaic, are the channels through which the connection is made. Viewing them can be likened to dialing the right telephone number, or typing in the correct codes to run a computer program. The connection is established at the metaphysical level of our being and radiates into our physical plane of existence, but first there is the metaphysical "fixing." Through positive thoughts and actions, we have to consciously permit the immense power of the Zohar to radiate love, harmony, and peace into our lives for us to share with all humanity and the universe.

As a work that has not only survived for millennia, but that is now much more widely read than ever before, we must credit the Zohar with some inner dynamic that staves off the forces of time. Indeed, immortality is a persistent theme in the text, and the Zohar itself seems to embody its own formula for eternal life. What is so unique about this document? What has permitted the Zohar to survive the powerful forces that for so long sought to suppress it?

The Zohar itself provides an answer to these questions. It is immortal as a book because immortality is humanity's destiny, to be achieved through the power of Kabbalah. The Zohar is the chief instrument of that power. As it is written: "And Moses said unto Rabbi Shimon bar Yochai, 'Only through your compendium, The

Zohar, shall humankind taste from the Tree-of-Life Reality.' " It could hardly be put any clearer. The Zohar has the power to redeem us, and to return us to paradise.

The Ten *Sefirot*: Emanations of the Divine

According to kabbalistic teaching, the creation of the universe was made possible by a withdrawal of the Light of the Creator, which was otherwise present everywhere. The reason for this withdrawal was for our own sake. The Creator knows that we cannot receive the full intensity of His Light. Therefore we are separated from God by a sequence of ten energy fields known as the *Sefirot* (singular, *Sefirah*).

Each *Sefirah* has distinctive properties, qualities, and, kabbalistically, lessons to be absorbed and mastered. Together, arranged in Right, Left, and Central Columns, the ten make up what kabbalists call "the Tree of Life." As we increase our spiritual competency by ascending each *Sefirah,* we simultaneously increase our spiritual capacity, giving us the ability to connect with and contain more and more Light. In other words, we are able to draw ever nearer to the Creator.

Like any tree, the Tree of Life emanates from its source (kabbalistically, its cause), that is, the original seed. Its roots stretch into the depths and its leaves and branches—the parts that are seen (its effects)—stretch upward. However, there is a difference. When we hold the image of a tree in our mind's eye, no doubt we see it with its roots sunk into the earth from whence it draws sustenance. The trunk rises from the ground and its branches grow upward and outward; its leaves form a crown of greenery. But true to paradox, which is virtually the cardinal rule of Kabbalah, the Tree of Life is a mirror image of our earthly tree. Its source is pure Spirit, the Creator's Light, and therefore its crown. The *Sefirah* called *Keter* is actually the Tree's roots, drawing sustenance from the Light. Its columns—Central, Right, and Left—reach downward toward our material world, the *Sefirah* called *Malchut*.

The *Sefirot* may be thought of as spiritual transformers, successively downgrading the Creator's infinite brightness until it reaches us in a manageable intensity in *Malchut;* the path traveled by the Light is depicted as the zigzagging trajectory of a bolt of lightning. As we transform our natures and increase the capacity of our spiritual vessel to hold Light, we, in essence, redraw that jagged path of Light back to its Source. In essence, we are climbing the tree to its roots!

And yet, it would be wrong to think of the ten *Sefirot* as external to ourselves because, paradoxically, they are both levels to be attained and also are all contained within us in potential form, ready to be awakened and mastered through our transformative spiritual work:

Not only are the *Sefirot* divided into three columns—Right (positive, masculine), Left (negative, feminine), and Central (mediating or balancing)—but they are also divided into four levels or "worlds." *Atzilut,* meaning "nearness" or "emanation," is made up of the *Sefirot Keter, Chochmah,* and *Binah.* Closest to the Creator, *Atzilut* is the purely spiritual realm. *Beriah,* meaning "creation," made up of the *Sefirot Chesed, Gvurah,* and *Tiferet,* is the realm of the intellect; *Yetzirah,* or "formation," made up of the *Sefirot Netzach, Hod,* and *Yesod,* is the emotional world; and *Assiyah,* meaning "action," is composed solely of our material plane, *Malchut,* the realm of physicality. But let us look at each of the *Sefirot* individually.

1. *Keter*

Keter is the summit of the Central Column, and as noted, it is paradoxically both the "crown" and the source. *Keter* represents the unknowable essence of the Creator. It marks the entryway to what Kabbalah calls "the Endless World," a dimension of unlimited

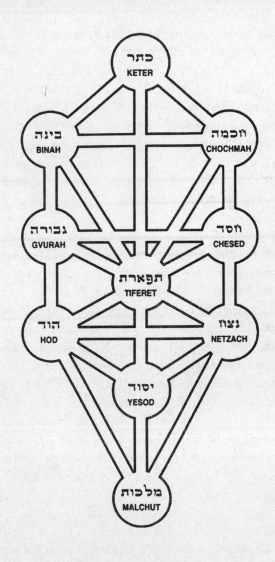

Light, far beyond human understanding. Here all exists in undifferentiated potential.

Keter is the blazing intelligence that channels the Light of the Creator to the rest of the Tree of Life.

2. Chochmah

As the highest level of the Right Column, *Chochmah* is the first *Sefirah* to receive the power that flows from the Endless World through *Keter*. *Chochmah* is recognized as the universal father figure, the primordial point of creation from which all knowable reality originates. It has the property of wisdom "beyond reason," that is, an inspired and pure knowing.

3. Binah

Topping the Left Column, *Binah* is considered to be the universal mother figure, and, complementing *Chochmah*'s knowing, it carries the property of understanding. *Binah* also contains all energy—from that which motivates human endeavor to that which keeps galaxies spinning. As *Chochma* and *Binah*, universal father and mother, meet, thought becomes manifest in action. Their combined energies are funneled through a "pseudo-*Sefirah*" called *Da'at*, which lies on the Central column below *Keter*. Even to kabbalists, *Da'at* is enigmatic, but while not regarded as a true *Sefirah*, it is thought to unify the energies of *Chochmah*'s wisdom and *Binah*'s understanding, transmitting them to the lower *Sefirot* as knowledge. (*Da'at* is frequently associated with the Tree of the Knowledge of Good and Evil that the Creator placed in the Garden of Eden along with the Tree of Life.)

4. Chesed

Below *Chochmah* on the Right Column, *Chesed* is the most expansive of the *Sefirot*. It contains the energy of mercy and the unrestricted desire to share. *Chesed* is also symbolic of the Sabbath, the Creator's gift of rest to us, a pause in our daily toil, and peace. *Chesed* represents the acts of loving-kindness that we humans can show one another. However, unbalanced, *Chesed* can be "generous to a fault," and undisciplined.

5. *Gvurah*

Opposite *Chesed*, on the Left Column, *Gvurah* carries the energy of judgment and restriction. It demands that there be consequences to our actions. It is a counterbalance to the overflowing generosity of *Chesed* and actually is the first significant block to our being overwhelmed by the Light of the Creator. It is here that the process of differentiation, the beginning of physicality originates. Associated with this *Sefirah* is the archangel Samael (the left hand of God), also known kabbalistically as "the Adversary." Unrestrained, the energy of *Gvurah* can become destructive.

6. *Tiferet*

Tiferet carries the energy of beauty and ideal balance—without such symmetry, in fact, there can be no beauty. Through this Central-Column *Sefirah,* the Light of the Creator is channeled downward and the spiritual aspirations of humankind are channeled upward. *Tiferet* may be thought of as the heart of the Tree of Life. As a balance between judgment and mercy, this *Sefirah* is associated with the patriarch Jacob. Here we find combined wisdom, understanding, and the luminosity of the Light.

7. *Netzach*

On the Right Column, below *Chesed, Netzach,* carrying the energy of "victory," resides. Like *Chesed, Netzach* radiates an expansive desire to share and brings that desire into physicality. This *Sefirah* represents the ideas of continuity and eternity. It is associated with

Moses, who as a link between the Creator and the people, personifies these enduring qualities. *Netzach* can be thought of as the sperm that, when united with an egg, carries specific qualities into the future via the birth of a new (yet "like") being. *Netzach* is associated with intuitive, involuntary, "right-brain" processes. It is the realm of the dreamer, the artist, and the masculine, fertilizing principle.

8. Hod

The Left-Column counterpart to *Netzach, Hod* ("glory") is analogous to the egg in human conception. *Hod,* which is also associated with prophecy, controls voluntary processes and left-brain activity, channeling the practicality of *Gvurah* into the human psyche. *Hod* is the feminine, or manifesting principle. It is here that the potentials held in the male aspects of *Chesed/Netzach* begin to become material. The dreams become concrete.

9. Yesod

At the base of the Tree of Life, this Central-Column *Sefirah* (called "foundation") sits like a great reservoir. All the *Sefirot* above pour their attributes into *Yesod*'s vast basin where they are mixed, balanced, and made ready to be channeled into the world of action. Although the Light has been channeled through eight other *Sefirot,* still, in *Yesod* its brilliance is beyond bearing to us in the physical world.

10. Malchut

Called by kabbalists "the Kingdom," *Malchut,* the lowest of the *Sefirot,* is the world of our material universe. To understand *Malchut* and its relationship to the other nine *Sefirot,* it may be helpful to think of it as a house. The house was conceived of by *Chochmah. Binah* provided the energy to build it. *Chesed* provided a loving willingness to build it. *Gvurah* calculated its measurements. *Tiferet* provided a lovely and level setting. *Netzach* supplied a color scheme, while *Hod* provided the building materials. *Yesod* dug a foundation.

Malchut is our home; it is the world we live in. It is the only one of the *Sefirot* where there is a perception of physicality. It is where the Tree of Knowledge of Good and Evil sinks its roots in a mirror image of the Tree of Life. And it is here that a divergence in human attitude spells the difference between lives lived in the Light, or in the darkness.

A Final Definition

I have used the term *kabbalist* several times in this introduction, and the term will appear often in the chapters that follow. Before going any further, therefore, there are several reasons why it is important to define this word. First, a careful definition will reveal the richness of a term that might otherwise seem honorific but vague, like "professor" or "doctor." In addition, from a practical viewpoint, by understanding what a kabbalist really is, we can understand what it is our opportunity to become. Kabbalah teaches that we will all eventually achieve this level of spiritual development. In that sense, the word not only reveals the greatness of those who have come before, but also the powers that are even now within ourselves.

When someone is described as a kabbalist, this denotes four specific aspects of being. Within the technical system of Kabbalah, for example, a kabbalist has advanced much further than an average person along the path of the *Sefirot*, the ten levels of illumination that ascend toward the Creator. Second, in terms of life in the material world, a kabbalist lives every day according to the teachings of Kabbalah and uses the spiritual tools of Kabbalah with complete certainty in their powers. He or she observes the rituals, recites the prayers, and follows the precepts that have been given to us by God. In addition, a kabbalist is traditionally a person who has received a heritage of teachings and wisdom from a master, who in turn received it from a still earlier master. In this sense, he or she is a living link with the biblical patriarchs and matriarchs, including not only Abraham, Isaac, and Jacob, but even Adam himself. Finally, a kabbalist is a teacher, who is committed not only to practicing Kabbalah but to helping others do the same—through study, writing, and, most of all, by living example.

NOTE: Throughout this book, passages from the Zohar are from *The Zohar: The First Ever Unabridged English Translation, with Commentary* (22 vols.), ed. Rabbi Michael Berg; published by The Kabbalah Centre, 2001. Within each chapter, citations by volume and page number of the Zohar are continuous until the appearance of a new citation, or until the end of the chapter. Some passages have been edited for this volume.

Part Two

TEACHINGS

CHAPTER I

NORTH OF THE NORTH POLE: CREATION AND WHAT CAME BEFORE

For almost a hundred years, there has been an ongoing revolution in how science looks at the creation of the universe and the direction, if any, that creation continues to follow. Theories have come and gone, while the "Theory of Everything" that would integrate quantum mechanics with relativity has remained elusive. For its part, Kabbalah not only describes what happened, what is happening, and what is going to happen, but also finds deep spiritual meaning in these events. Thus, from a kabbalistic point of view, the widely accepted Big Bang theory of creation is important not only for its narrative of physical events but also for what it teaches us about the issues of our lives, and how we should deal with them. The specific teachings pertaining to this form much of the content of this book.

Kabbalah and the Zohar not only deal with the Big Bang and its consequences but also engage one of the most vexing questions that has yet been put to modern science. Physics and cosmology describe the universe coming into being when an infinitely dense mass, currently thought to have been about the size of a dime, exploded outward with inconceivable force—the Big Bang. But what preceded the Big Bang? Where did the dime-sized entity come from? Who or what put it all together?

To some, this is a naive question. The physicist Stephen

Hawking, for example, declared that asking what came before the Big Bang is like asking what is north of the North Pole. On the other hand, an equally eminent scientist, the late Richard Feynman, believed that an inability to respond to "naive" questions is a serious weakness for a scientist or anyone else. Kabbalah most definitely has a response and, like the universe itself, it is still evolving.

The Zohar describes the "beginning of the beginning" in the following passage:

Vol. 1, p. 226

With the beginning of the manifestation of the Creator's will—that is, when the Creator desired to create the world—a hard spark made an engraving upon the supernal Light. This hard spark emanated from the most concealed of all concealed things—from the *Ein Sof*—and took a shapeless form. The spark was then inserted into the center of a circle that was neither white nor black nor red nor green, nor any color at all. When He began its measurements, He created bright colors that shone into the empty space and the engraving. From within this hard spark a fountain spouted, from which the shades down below received their colors.

These lines have been closely explicated over many centuries, and most significantly by the great kabbalist Rabbi Isaac Luria, who from these words inferred the concept of *tzimtzum*, which can be translated as "contraction" or "self-limitation." Rabbi Luria's teaching refers not to the creation of the physical universe, but to an even earlier, primordial event that was necessary for creation to become possible. Kabbalists since the sixteenth century have interpreted and elaborated upon Rabbi Luria's insights. The twentieth-century kabbalist Rabbi Yehuda Ashlag (translator of portions of the Zohar from Aramaic into Hebrew), in his book *Ten Luminous Emanations,* presents what may be regarded as the completion or fulfillment of the *tzimtzum* concept.

Why did we have to wait until the twentieth century to penetrate the secrets of the universe? The answer is simple: Rabbi Ashlag lived in the twentieth century. His efforts were necessary to unveil the subconscious realm of the universe by revealing the concealed wisdom of Kabbalah and thus turning the Light on, the Light of Kabbalah. The veils, limitations, and illusions of the conscious mind then began to disappear. The Light began to take its rightful place in our universe. This prompted the remarkable and wondrous theories, discoveries, and new technological achievements with which we have been blessed. The limitations of the physical world—time, space, motion—are falling away.

How could something so immense be so simple? If we think of electric light, we can understand the sudden transformation. A mere flip of the light switch transforms a dark room, whether it be a tiny closet or an immense auditorium. This act of turning on the Light, so central in Kabbalah, is recognized in all spiritual teachings. All religions have their kabbalist.

Humanity has been pondering the Zohar for millennia, struggling to unravel its secrets and penetrate its codes. But with little or no success. At last, Rabbi Ashlag has removed the cloak and unveiled the mysteries. And when the Light goes on, previously unrealized and unseen discoveries are noticed. They were there all the time. We just could not see them in the darkness.

Nothing is more important for the new Kabbalah student than a sound understanding of Rabbi Ashlag's ideas, all of which are contained or concealed in the preceding Zohar passage. Before we undertake a careful reading of that passage, therefore, it will be helpful to look at Rabbi Ashlag's contemporary explication, and then to work backward to the original Zohar text, which might otherwise seem hopelessly obscure.

Rabbi Ashlag begins with the premise that, before the creation of *anything*—not only the physical world, but even the dimensions of time and space—the positive energy of God was everywhere present. In Hebrew, this energy is called *Or* (Light), and further discussion will show why this is an extremely apt designation. Although it is tempting to attach an emotional component to this positive energy—to call it "love," for example—the many connotations of such poetic words argue for a less encumbered terminology. In any case, the energy of the Creator was not love in the sense of affection for an object, because there was no object—and this was the problem. At its essence, the Creator's nature is one of sharing: a desire to give of itself. But when there was nothing to receive the giving intention, a reciprocal energy had to come into being to complete the circuitry. In kabbalistic terms, a Vessel was needed to accept the Light.

And a Vessel *was* created. The primordial Vessel embodied an entirely new energy—the energy of receiving. Being the exact opposite of, or complementary to, the Creator's sharing essence, the Vessel allowed His essence to be fulfilled. Kabbalists maintain that the appearance of the Vessel was the only "out of nothing" creation that has ever taken place in this or any universe.

The creation of the Vessel was by no means the end, however. It was not even the beginning, or the beginning of the beginning. A dialectical process had started, one whose continuation was implied by a fundamental duality in the Vessel's nature. Although the Vessel was created only to receive, because it was formed of God's sharing energy, which was heretofore ubiquitous, the Vessel also contained an x-factor of sharing, like a gene buried deep within its biological programming.

As the Vessel received the Light, an aspect of its dual nature began to amplify. Contemporary kabbalists compare this to a glass growing warmer as hot liquid is poured into it: The receiver (the glass) expresses the character (warmth) of what is received. Or, at least, that is what the Vessel "wanted." Keeping in mind the limits to which we can attribute human emotions to primordial events, we can say that the Vessel, in addition to receiving, now desired to express the giving intention that, after all, comprised much of its essential makeup. It "wanted" to give as well as get. It "wanted" to be like the Creator. Indeed, its real desire was for nothing less than unity with the all-giving God.

The kabbalistic doctrine known as *Bread of Shame* tells us that the Vessel felt shame at the one-sidedness of its relationship with the Creator. The Creator's wish and sole purpose was to bestow abundance on His creations. But His creations could partake of His abundance only to the degree that their sense of unearned largesse would allow them. Kabbalah teaches that there can be "no coercion in spirituality." The experience of earning fulfillment is an essential part of fulfillment itself.

It was now, in Rabbi Ashlag's narrative, that the Vessel *pushed back* against the Light—and the Light, obliging the Vessel's desire for separation, withdrew. It contracted. It restricted itself. This was the event that Rabbi Luria called the *tzimtzum*.

The duality of the Vessel had expressed itself. It had not, however, *resolved* itself. At the risk of another possibly vulgarizing analogy, we can compare the Vessel to an adolescent who, out of desire for independence, runs away from home and then misses a warm bed at night. Kabbalah teaches that the Vessel instantly wanted or needed the Light's return with the same primal force that causes a vacuum to be filled, a bubble to burst, or a swollen river to overflow its banks. The violence of these images is consciously chosen, because although the Vessel needed the Light, it was unprepared to accept the sudden return of the Light at full force. When the Light did reconnect with the Vessel, one of the central events of Kabbalah occurred. The Vessel shattered—and at that instant the line between physical and metaphysical realities was crossed once and for all. Kabbalah teaches that the shattering of the Vessel is identical with the Big Bang of modern physics. Just as all matter in the physical world is a legacy of the Big Bang, all spirituality is a legacy of the shattering of the Vessel.

It is a beautiful formulation. It is also, at least as we have so far described it, an oversimplification of both the physical and spiritual realities—because the nature of those realities is much more closely interwoven than we ordinarily imagine. When we imagine the Big Bang, for example, we think of the primordial entity as exploding outward into space. But space was contained within the object itself, as was time. There could be no explosion "out" or "into" because those concepts came into being at the same instant as the explosion itself. Within the intangible and metaphysical realms of our minds, fractions of seconds have no meaning. It is well worth noting that, in a similar way, mental processes take place outside any concept of time. In the mind, as in the primordial realm and the quantum dimension, notions of past, present, and future do not exist. And what we think of as material reality is, at its origin, no more or less tangible than time or space, which we construe as intangible and abstract. This is a very important realization, especially in Kabbalah, which sees the remnants of the shattered Vessel literally everywhere, from the physical objects that furnish our houses to the emotional and spiritual inclinations that so complicate our hearts.

With all this in mind, we can now consider the enigmatic Zohar passage quoted earlier: "With the beginning of the manifestation of the Creator's will. . . ." In line with the ambiguous nature of tangible and intangible realities, which Kabbalah understood long before natural science, the passage deals with both matter and consciousness.

It concerns matter in the sense that it refers to actual events that brought about the physical world. The Zohar is describing the origin of *everything*, including this book, the roof over your head, and the human body your soul now inhabits. The process recounted here is not a metaphor, just as the patriarchs and matriarchs of the Bible are not mere symbols of particular points of view or levels of spiritual development. They were actual flesh and blood human beings. This is a crucial point. Unless kabbalistic teachings are understood to originate in historical reality—albeit a reality far removed from the one we inhabit today—Kabbalah may be construed as mere "philosophy." The primordial events described here are not just visionary exercises in the mind of the author or the reader. They really happened.

But if this passage is a description of the actual events that foreshadowed the creation of the material world, to the lay reader it may seem an incomplete and even an inadequate rendering—as if the words were being called upon to express the inexpressible. To a new Kabbalah student, a phrase such as "a hard spark emanated from the most concealed of all concealed things ... and took a shapeless form" can suggest that the real intention is not to create a visual image but to highlight the fundamental impossibility of creating one. One may feel this at many places in the Zohar, whether the subject is the apparent triumph of wickedness in the world or the unlimited benevolence of the Creator. These questions, however, arise from a literary reading of the Zohar rather than a kabbalistic one. The Zohar presents us with mysteries, but they are never simply dead ends. When a chapter or even a phrase is enigmatic, we are meant to use the tools of Kabbalah to penetrate them.

Some of these tools may take time to acquire. They can include a knowledge of the Hebrew language, and perhaps the kabbalistic system of numerological interpretation known as *gematria*. Most important of all is the level of the reader's own consciousness. As we learn to live Kabbalah and not just to "understand" it, the mysteries of the Zohar open themselves to us, as do the mysteries of life itself.

CHAPTER 2

FEAR, AWE, AND LOVE OF GOD

In our daily lives, fear has a bad name. "We have nothing to fear but fear itself," said President Franklin Roosevelt during the worst days of the Great Depression, and he was hardly the first to identify fear as the foundation of negativity. Yet kabbalistic teachings on fear are more complex. The sages counsel us to see beyond the apparent dangers of the moment and to trust in the Creator's power to deliver us. Yet in another context Kabbalah depicts fear in a very positive light—not all fear, of course, but the specific inner state referred to as fear of the Creator.

In the collection of kabbalistic writings entitled *The Ways of the Tzaddikim,* first published more than four hundred years ago, a striking reference to this kind of fear occurs: "The beginning of all knowledge is fear of the Creator." This echoes the biblical passage, "The fear of the Lord is the beginning of wisdom." (Job 28:28) The phrase also recalls the dictum of Socrates, who linked fear and knowledge when he defined courage as "knowing what to fear."

At first glance, this seems puzzling. Is Socrates telling us that courage and fear are somehow bound together? Are the sages of Kabbalah counseling fear of the Creator at the same time as they implore us to trust Him? Kabbalistically, however, the fear of God is something very different from fear of bad investments or long checkout lines. Fear of God is simply an acknowledgment of the supreme source of wisdom, energy, and Light. In this sense, fear of God frees us from fear in any other form. We fear the Creator not with sweaty palms and shortness of breath, but with a clear understanding that the Creator is the ultimate source of strength in the universe. By fearing the Creator, and only the Creator, we are liberated. We gain the power to face any obstacle with calm and trust.

Vol. 1, pp. 188–194

"In the beginning, the Creator created." This is the first and foremost of all precepts. And it is called *fear of the Creator*, which is "the beginning." As it is written, "fear of the Creator is the beginning of wisdom," and "the beginning of knowledge." It is the gateway through which one enters the realm of faith. The very existence of the world is based on this precept.

Fear of the Creator is divided into three categories. Two of these have no real source or basis, and the third is the authentic foundation of fear. In the first category, a man may fear and respect the Creator in the hope that his sons will live and not die, or because he fears punishment through loss of his health or his possessions in this world. The second category includes people who fear punishment in the next world. Neither of these two categories of fear come from an authentic source.

He whose fear is based on the possibility of punishment lacks the fear of the Creator that leads to life. Such a man is ruled by "evil fear," and the punishment for this transgression is the cruel lash. It is written, "The Creator created the heavens and the earth; and the earth was without form and void, and the darkness was upon the face of the deep; and the 'spirit' of Elohim." These are the four punishments of the wicked.

Without form means strangulation. *Void* means stoning and refers to the stones that are sunk in the great deep for the purpose of punishing the wicked. *Darkness* means burning, as it is written, "And it came to pass when you heard the voice out of the midst of the darkness, while the mountain did burn with fire." (Deuteronomy 5:20) This fierce fire "shall fall upon the heads of the wicked." (Jeremiah 23:19) *Spirit* means slaughtering by the sword, as it is written, "the bright blade of a burning sword." (Genesis 3:24) This is also called the spirit. This is the punishment for whomever transgresses the precepts of the Torah.

Genuine fear exists when we fear the Creator because He is almighty and governs over all; because He is the source and essence of all worlds.

This is the foundation and the most important principle of all the Torah's precepts. Whoever observes the precept of fear observes all the others, and whoever ignores the precept of fear does not observe any of the precepts of the Torah. Fear of the Creator is the gateway to everything!

No idea in Kabbalah is more important than the true meaning of fear. The importance accorded to fear is shared by many ancient philosophies, a number of which were almost certainly influenced by kabbalistic doctrine. To Aristotle, for example, courage is the basis of all virtue. It is the one that makes all others possible, and also the one, when absent, that renders us incapable of any positive action. And courage, of course, cannot be understood except in terms of its opposite. Thus, the classical philosophers defined courage as "knowing what to fear," an insight that accords perfectly with the preceding Zohar text.

These passages raise several important questions that are easily open to misunderstanding. Most important, is fear really the word the sages meant to apply to our relationship with the Creator? If the essence of God is love and sharing, what is there to be afraid of? I believe there is a real contradiction here, and for this reason I believe a distinction should be made between fear and *awe*. The basis of this distinction can be stated quite simply: Fear is a painful emotion associated with a vision of the future that might happen; awe is a positive sensation associated with something that already is.

When the Zohar divides fear into three types, a linguistic issue comes into play. It can be resolved by referring to the final category of fear as *awe*. This seems very appropriate, since the two opening classifications differ from each other only in their object, but both are fundamentally different from the third.

In the first instance, for example, a man fears God because he does not want to lose the things that make him comfortable and happy on earth. He is afraid illness might strike his family, and he identifies that fear with the Creator. He doesn't want his house to burn down, and he is afraid God might inflict that upon him. Health and home are very human needs, and perhaps we ourselves have experienced fear of losing these in whatever measure we currently enjoy them. But when we do feel such fears, we should realize that in fearing we have essentially made ourselves hostage to the vicissitudes of life in the real world. We have bound our happiness to the well-being of people and things whose very natures are vulnerable and even perishable. When the Zohar refers to this as an inauthentic category of fear, it means that the emotion does not derive from anything that is truly fundamental to our being. Much as we might care for our own health, our family, or our house, they are appendages to our existence, not the basis of it. As long as we are afraid of losing those things, and as long as we make that fear the motivation for our relationship to God, we cannot truly reveal His Light.

The second category of fear simply moves the object of dread from this world to the next. Instead of beseeching the Creator to spare our real estate and our bank accounts, we implore Him to keep us out of hell. The distinction between the first type of fear to this one is the difference between Kabbalah's depiction of ancient Egypt and the repressive theocracies of Calvinist Geneva or Puritan New England. In the former, Kabbalah teaches there was a blatant pursuit of physicality, motivated by desire to receive for the self alone. In the latter, condemnation of materialism in this world became the pretext for a fixation on punishment in the world to come. According to Kabbalah, this can in no sense be considered progress. Fear of losing the keys to heaven is no better than fear of losing the keys to the new Mercedes. In both cases we are dominated by negative expectation. Our prayers and observances become mere attempts to manipulate God. It is difficult to imagine anything more wrongheaded than that!

The Zohar enumerates four punishments for this wrongheadedness, and they are derived from the words of the biblical creation story: *without form, void, darkness, spirit.* These no more refer to physical torments of a conventional hell than the Buddha's Fire Sermon is a literal description of a world in flames. The Zohar is referring to the internal conditions that we inflict on ourselves through "evil fear," which is simply an incorrect understanding of our relationship to the Creator.

What is being said here is worth a close look, because, as always in Kabbalah, evil is condemned not in moral terms, but as a violation of the sound structural principles of the universe. Here "evil fear" is represented as an undoing of God's handiwork. "Evil fear" is regressive. It is unevolved. It is making a mess of something beautiful. It is an affront to the Creator almost in an aesthetic sense.

I am fond of describing Kabbalah as a set of tools for helping us gain fulfillment, transformation, and oneness with the Creator. To use the tools effectively, one needs to be aware of the "instructions": that is, the teachings offered in the Zohar and the other writings, and in the words and deeds of righteous men and women. Choosing not to employ the tools in the way they were designed and intended, or perhaps choosing not to use them at all brings about the chaos that the Zohar describes through metaphors of suffocation, stoning, burning, and slaughtering. It is not the Creator who inflicts these punishments on us; *we inflict them on ourselves*. Dante, in his *Divine Comedy*, thoroughly developed this concept of "poetic justice" through the sinners' punishments in the *Inferno*. Perhaps Dante even read the Zohar, which was rediscovered by Rabbi Moses de Leon at about the same time that *The Divine Comedy* was composed. An important Buddhist text entitled *The Questions of King Milinda* also includes the idea of self-inflicted punishments by the wicked. Perhaps this is something the human imagination has always understood, which in turn makes the persistence of evil even more difficult to understand. Escaping it should be so easy, yet in actuality it is impossibly difficult for so many. An important difference between Dante and the Zohar is the kabbalistic teaching that salvation and transformation are always available, at every instant, no matter how far we may have fallen. The *Inferno* presents much that accords with Kabbalah, but Dante's idea that condemned sinners are without hope is absolutely contradicted by Kabbalah. In fact, the kabbalists explain that the loss of hope is one of the most powerful weapons of the negative side of our nature. We can always free ourselves. Even at the last instant of life, we can always open ourselves to the sense of awe that the Zohar describes as sustaining "the very existence of the world."

Awe of the Creator is a profoundly spiritual experience, and it is also a thoroughly reasonable one. It is seeing things as they really are. As the Zohar puts it, we feel awe before God "because He is almighty and governs over all; because he is the source and essence of all worlds." What is so difficult about this? Why do people resist it? What possible reason could there be for refusing to acknowledge the greatness of God, and thereby to receive the true fulfillment that He has ordained for us?

John Milton, in his characterization of Satan in *Paradise Lost,* lays out a map of the spiritual universe that accords well with kabbalistic teachings. Milton presents Satan as an overwhelmingly prideful personality who refuses to accept the supremacy of the Creator, even when he recognizes this supremacy as plain fact. To achieve his desired level of self-aggrandizement, he is determined to assert that two plus two makes five. There is something deeply self-destructive about this, which is of course the ultimate attraction.

As the Zohar makes clear, we must open ourselves to awe of the Creator as the precondition of living according to the precepts of Torah. As the Zohar expresses it, "Awe of the Creator is the gateway to everything!" What a powerful sentence that is, and what a mystery that humanity finds it so difficult to pass through that door.

Following its exploration of fear and awe, the Zohar discusses the importance of love for God, which it presents as a closely related precept:

A person should love the Creator truly and perfectly. As it is written, "Walk before me and be perfect." (Genesis 17:1)

Rabbi Elazar said: "Perfect love is perfected from both sides, that is, from kindness and from judgment. This is true and proper love.

"There are people who love the Creator because they are rich, because they have length of life, because their children are around them, because they rule their enemies, and because they succeed in all their ventures. But if the Creator were to revolve the wheel of fortune and replace these gifts with harsh judgment, they would turn against Him. Therefore this love lacks foundation."

Rabbi Shimon came and kissed Rabbi Elazar and blessed him. He then said: "Certainly the Creator has sent me here. This is the tiny ray of light that I was told shines in my house, and later shall light the whole world." Rabbi Elazar said: "Certainly fear should be attached to the precept of love. How is it attached? When the Creator gives a person riches, length of life, children, and sustenance, then that person should arouse fear in himself. He should be afraid of what sin might bring upon him, causing the wheel of fortune to turn! Of this it is written, happy is the man that fears always (Proverbs 28:14), because fear is now included with love."

Our purpose in the world is to gain joy and fulfillment though unity with the Creator. This purpose never changes. It is unaffected by the material conditions of our lives, including the state of our health. An Olympic athlete and a permanently disabled victim of an automobile crash are both moving toward the same goal. For the moment, they are just traveling along different routes.

Our relationship to the Creator in many ways resembles a marriage—in its complexity, its intimacy, and most of all in its inclusiveness. Everyone knows the lines of the traditional Protestant marriage ceremony: "In sickness or in health . . . for richer or for poorer." Surprisingly, this is not how the lines actually read. In an accurate rendition, *or* is replaced by *and,* which changes the meaning dramatically. Now the ups and downs of a life together are presented not just as possibilities, but as certainties. From a kabbalistic viewpoint, this is all to the good. Reversals of fortune are opportunities for growth. A relationship that exists under a set of unchanging conditions can hardly be called complete—and *complete* is what the Zohar means by *perfect.*

The kabbalists tell us that the Creator loves us unconditionally. He sees us at our worst moments, and His love never falters. To achieve our purpose of oneness with His nature, we must be able to return His love under conditions of judgment as well as those of mercy. If we really believe in the Light as all-loving and good, we cannot see ourselves as victims whenever a problem arises, regardless of how painful it might be. We must take responsibility in accepting the obstacle as an occasion for positive change, and also as an opportunity to exercise our certainty of God's love even under difficult circumstances, or even truly terrible ones.

When the Zohar cautions us to be fearful when things are going well, this does not mean that we should buy a hedge fund or keep money hidden under the mattress. Rather, it urges us to maintain the completeness of our relationship with God even when only one aspect of that relationship is now expressed on the material level. Even when our lives are filled "with goodness and mercy," as the psalmist puts it, we should keep awareness of judgment alive in our hearts for the same reason that awareness of pain allows us to experience pleasure. Similarly, when judgment does take place, we should remember all that is merciful in our lives as well.

> "The Light of Creation is first revealed, then hidden and treasured. When it is hidden, harsh judgment comes forth and both aspects—kindness and judgment—become united and reach perfection."

In this short verse, the Zohar reprises not only the primordial events leading to Creation but also the arc of our own lives, from blindness in the overwhelming Light, to darkness, and finally to wisdom and transformation. At first the Light of the Creator was fully revealed; it was everywhere. Then it withdrew. It created a distance between itself and the material realm—not a physical distance, but a spiritual one that it is our task to bridge over the course of a lifetime. Among the biblical patriarchs, it is Jacob who personifies this journey, and it is he who opened the channels through which we can negotiate it in our own lives. Jacob's grandfather was Abraham, who was a pure being of kindness and mercy. Jacob's father was Isaac, who embodied the reciprocal quality of severity and judgment. During his lifetime, and especially through his wrestling with the angel on the night before confronting his brother Esau, Jacob became the expression of *Tiferet*, the divine emanation of perfect harmony.

We can accomplish this for ourselves by employing the divinely given tools of Kabbalah. But we must learn to use and trust them in sickness *and* in health, in riches *and* in poverty, in love *and* in awe of the God. With these tools, we can resolve the apparent opposition between mercy and fear. We can, as the Zohar tells us, reach synthesis, unity, and perfection.

CHAPTER 3

RABBI YOSI AND TORAH STUDY

T his story introduces one of the Zohar's central characters together with some of Kabbalah's most important
teachings. To understand it, we must begin with the
concept of Torah as much more than either a written document or
an oral tradition of learning and wisdom. Torah in the context of
this story simply means *truth*. When Rabbi Aba speaks of studying
Torah, he means turning our minds, our hearts, and our actions
toward the ultimate truth that God is One.

Nothing could be more absurd than linking this truth to any
sort of material gain, as Yosi explicitly does in the story's opening
paragraph. This is the point of Rabbi Aba's instruction that henceforth Rabbi Yosi should be referred to as "a man of great wealth." It
is an instruction that is at once humorous and profound. In one
sense it is comical to suggest that Yosi's desire for wealth can be
served just by having everyone suddenly refer to him as wealthy. Yet
is this not also exactly what "wealth" really demands? It is not the
physical sensation of money passing through his hands that Yosi
wishes for. It is recognition in the eyes of others that he is a rich
man. By showing him how easily available this is, Rabbi Aba also
shows exactly how much it is really worth.

Rabbi Aba declared that whoever desires to be rich and have a long life in the world to come should study Torah. One day a bachelor in Rabbi Aba's neighborhood said to him, "Rabbi, I wish to study Torah so that I may become wealthy." Rabbi Aba responded, "What is your name?" The bachelor said, "Yosi." Rabbi Aba told his pupils henceforth to refer to the bachelor as, "Yosi, a man of great wealth." And Yosi devoted himself to the study of Torah.

Time passed. One day Yosi stood before Rabbi Aba and asked, "Where is the wealth?" Rabbi Aba responded, "I can see you are not studying for the sake of heaven!" He returned to his room to consider what to do with Yosi, and there he heard a voice that said: Do not punish him, because he shall become a great man! So Rabbi Aba returned to Yosi and said, "Sit down, my son, and I shall give you wealth."

Before long a man arrived who had a vessel made of pure gold. He showed it to everyone, and its sparkle lit up the whole house. The man said to Rabbi Aba, "Rabbi, I wish to merit understanding of Torah. But because I myself have not merited this understanding, I am searching for someone who can learn Torah for my sake. I inherited great wealth from my father, who used to set upon his table thirteen of these cups made of pure gold. I wish to achieve the great merit of studying Torah, and I shall give my wealth to achieve it."

Rabbi Aba said to Yosi, "Study Torah, and this man

shall give you wealth!" Whereupon the man gave Yosi the golden cup, and Rabbi Aba spoke aloud the verse, "Gold and crystal cannot equal it, and the exchange of it shall not be for vessels of fine gold." Yosi the bachelor then sat down and studied Torah, while the other man gave him wealth.

As time passed, the desire for Torah entered Yosi's bowels. One day, Rabbi Aba found him in tears and asked, "Why are you weeping?" Yosi replied, "What am I losing in order to gain this wealth? Life in the world to come! I do not want to learn anymore for the sake of this man, but rather to merit Torah for myself." Rabbi Aba thought: "Now I understand that he is studying for the sake of heaven."

He called for that man and said, "Take your wealth back and share it with the poor and the orphans. I shall give you a bigger portion in the Torah, from which we all are learning!" Yosi returned the cup of gold to him, and to this very day the name the *son of gold* has not been taken away from him or from his children. He became the famous Rabbi Yosi ben Pazi. He and his sons merited much Torah, for there is no greater reward in the world than to study Torah.

This is a lesson that could hardly have been made more powerfully or concisely. As the text continues, it develops into an account of personal transformation as well as an allegory of human desire and the means of authentically fulfilling it.

According to the ancient wisdom of Kabbalah, reality diminishes in direct proportion to physicality. Deluged by an endless stream of sensory stimulation, we may easily be deceived into thinking that the realm of appearances—the world we see, hear, taste, touch, and smell—is the sum total of existence. By challenging that assumption, we create a circuit with the Upper World and become a channel for higher states of consciousness. The kabbalist seeks neither to ignore the desires presented in this world, nor to satisfy them. He seeks to *restrict* them, to use their energy as a starting point for true self-determination.

When Rabbi Aba goes to his room to consider what to do about Yosi, whose Torah studies are improperly motivated by a yearning for material wealth, he has a revelation that a larger spiritual process is being worked out. Specifically, he is told not to punish Yosi, and in fact Aba merely sits down with him and tells him, "I will give you what you want." He might have said, "I'll first give you what you *think* you want, and then you'll get what you really want."

Then consider the man who brings his father's gold cup to Rabbi Aba. Whenever an unnamed person appears in the Zohar, his freedom from the limits of conventional identity is intended to signify his high stature. He may be a great sage, or, as here, he may be an angel who has materialized for a specific purpose—in this case, to assist in Yosi's spiritual transformation.

Aside from his anonymity, the angel also reveals his supernal stature in other ways. His humility, for example, suggests an elevated being. While he asserts that he does not merit Torah study, he is not deluded about his apparent material wealth. In this sense he is almost the opposite of Yosi, who neither questions his own worthiness to study nor doubts the value of material reward.

As the Zohar portrays him at the start of this chapter, Yosi really wants to be a magician rather than a kabbalist. Magic, according to Kabbalah, is a formidable power. It differs from true spirituality less in terms of what it can accomplish than in the ego-driven intention that lies behind it.

Magic is always about getting something rather than giving anything. It is the mirror image of spirituality, and like a real image in a mirror, it shrinks and reverses the subject. It should come as no surprise that Egypt was the center of magical practices in the biblical world, for in the Bible Egypt is portrayed as an unrelentingly materialist society.

It is also true, however, that "Egypt" is an internal state of being that we must pass through to achieve freedom and transformation. This is what we witness in Yosi. He is by no means an evil person, but simply a spiritually undeveloped one. The experience he goes through is the same maturation process that each of us faces individually, and that all humanity must also confront. Materialism is not unequivocally bad. It is like any childishly destructive behavior. It can be accepted and understood as a stage toward higher development.

Yosi is a kind of Faust. He wants to make a bargain that will fulfill his fantasies of wealth and power. Fortunately for him, he makes the bargain with Rabbi Aba rather than the devil. Fortunately, also, the angel who appears for Yosi's benefit is a true creature of sharing. Notice that he refers to his father—that is, the Creator—as having thirteen golden vessels. Kabbalah teaches that the number twelve represents completion. When the Bible refers to Job as the owner of eleven thousand sheep, this is a coded reference to his yet-to-be achieved spiritual fulfillment. Similarly, the angel's allusion to thirteen vessels denotes the overwhelming abundance of the Upper Worlds. The golden color of the vessels suggests the Light of the Creator, which is His presence in the physical world. Yosi's tears, too, are symbolically important. Tears shed with real sincerity foster an instant and powerful connection with the Creator. In a sense, they are an especially powerful kind of prayer that expresses itself beyond the limits of language.

The themes of this chapter—that the magic of transformation

is in the sharing rather than the receiving; that the righteous may present themselves as the unworthy; that to study Torah (truth) is a high honor, a blessing and its own reward—occur again and again in the Zohar and other kabbalistic texts. These are themes that we will refer to many times throughout this book.

CHAPTER 4

THE DONKEY DRIVER:
CONCEALMENT AND REVELATION

W e live in an age that celebrates speed, focus, practicality, and ease of use. At least at first glance, the
Zohar seems to offer none of these things. Over-
all, it is moving in the opposite direction from the cerebral, Aristotelian tradition that has dominated Western thought in general,
and that was the basis for some of the most influential books in
the Jewish tradition, such as Maimonides' *Guide for the Perplexed*.
Though in the opening volumes it follows the chronology of the
biblical narrative in a general way, the Zohar does not begin with the
Creation, and passages dealing with specific incidents often double
back on material that has already been covered, or invoke ideas and
characters that have not yet been introduced. There is a great deal of
material about Adam, fully as much about Noah and Abraham,
somewhat less about Isaac, quite a bit about Jacob and Joseph,
and much about Moses scattered here and there. Always there is a
tone of intimate connection with the biblical personalities, so that
we seem to be reading about the members of a family—our own
family—rather than remote patriarchs of a spiritual tradition.

The characteristically zoharic parts, however, are not usually
about these people, but concern the rabbis on their travels talking
about biblical verses and having epiphanies. An essential story of
this kind is this one about a donkey driver, which also concerns the

49

key theme of anonymity. Other key chapters concern soul mates and how to find them, the feminine presence for both good and ill, marriage and children, sexual practices, and the parting of the Red Sea.

The fairly informal style of commentary in these pages reflects that of the Zohar itself. In the terminology of philosophy, the Zohar is the opposite of Thomistic or Aristotelian. As was said of Emily Dickinson's poetry, reading it is like taking a walk across a field and finding many artifacts, some of which are complete pieces, and some are shards broken in very interesting ways.

The truth in Kabbalah is rarely what it seems, and often is the very opposite of what it seems. Again and again the text cautions against obvious interpretations, not only of the biblical writings, but of other people's and of our own lives as well. This story of a journey by two kabbalists is a case in point:

Vol. 1, pp. 125–134

Rabbi Elazar, the son of Rabbi Shimon bar Yochai, traveled with Rabbi Aba to visit Rabbi Yosi. Another man traveled with them. He walked behind them leading their donkeys.

Beginning with the Creator's command to Abraham that he "go forth from his own country," Kabbalah interprets every journey as an inner experience. Abraham's departure is understood as a breaking away from his present state of spiritual development, his "comfort zone," in order to open new channels of Light for himself and all humanity. In the same way, the setting forth of the two rabbis should be understood as a spiritual journey more than a physical one—the more so since these travelers are great scholars with a worthy destination. Moreover, they do not waste their time in idle conversation.

As they walked, Rabbi Aba said, "Let us begin a discussion of the Torah, for the time and place are propitious, and our talk can help us complete our journey."

Rabbi Elazar opened the discussion with the phrase, "*You shall keep my Shabbatot* [plural form of *Shabbat*]. Come and see: the Creator made the world in six days. But the first three days were all undisclosed and nothing appeared. But as soon as the fourth day arrived, He revealed His action and shared His strength with all!

"So Water, Fire, and Air—which are *Chesed, Gvurah,* and *Tiferet*—which are Right Column, Left Column, and Central Column—were kept in suspense and the full action of Creation was not revealed until the Earth—which is *Malchut*—disclosed them. . . ."

Chesed (kindness), *Gvurah* (strength), and *Tiferet* (balance) are three of the *Sefirot*, three emanations of the Creator's Light. But these remain hidden until the appearance of Earth, or *Malchut*, which Kabbalah associates with the principle of structure. Much to Rabbi Elazar's surprise, just as he introduces this notion the donkey driver brings up a point of scriptural exegesis.

The man who was driving the donkeys and following behind asked, "What is the meaning of, *And you shall revere my sanctuary?*"

Rabbi Aba replied: "This applies to the sanctity of the Shabbat."

Then the donkey driver asked, "And what is the sanctity of the Shabbat?"

Rabbi Aba replied, "It is the holiness that descends from above and rests upon the *Shabbat*. If the holiness that descends from above is called 'honorable,' it may seem as though the *Shabbat* itself is not honorable. Yet it is written, *'and you shall honor it.'* So the *Shabbat* in itself is honorable!"

Rabbi Elazar then said to Rabbi Aba, "Leave this man alone, for he has something wise to say, something of which we know nothing."

The donkey driver began, *"My Shabbatot* refers to both the higher *Shabbat* and the lower *Shabbat,* which are joined as one.

"Another *Shabbat,* however, remained unmentioned and felt humiliated. He told her: 'my daughter, now I am adorning you with a more glorious crown.' And this is the *Shabbat* of the eve of *Shabbat,* where fear and awe prevail. And I, the donkey driver, heard this from my father."

Consistent with the principle that what is concealed is more powerful than what is disclosed, the promise (that is, the eve) of *Shabbat* occupies a different spiritual category than the Sabbath itself.

The rabbis said to him: "Who has put you here to be a donkey driver?"

He replied: "The letter *Yud* waged war against the two letters *Chaf* and *Samech* to come and join me. But *Chaf* did not want to leave its place in the throne of the Creator. And the *Samech* did not want to leave its place supporting those who fall."

He continued: "The letter *Yud* came over to me, kissed me, embraced me, and wept together with me. It said to me, 'my son, what shall I do with you? I am leaving you to load myself with an abundance of good things and with a plenitude of precious, sublime, and secret letters. While I accomplish this purpose, my son, go and drive the donkeys.' And that is why I am still doing so!"

Kabbalah's understanding of the significance of the Hebrew letters is quite unlike our notion of the English alphabet. It is a principle of modern linguistics, for example, that the relationship between a word and the world is essentially arbitrary; there is nothing "doggier" about the word *dog* than there is about the word *cat*. But Hebrew words and the letters from which they are formed are much more than mere symbols. Each letter is like an element of the periodic table, with individual properties of density and conductivity. *Yud*, the tenth letter of the Hebrew alphabet, is an especially potent form of spiritual energy. Being the smallest letter, as we might expect in Kabbalah it also contains the greatest power. Like a subatomic particle of quantum physics, it is immune to the limits of time and space. It is understood as an energy of transition and new beginning.

Rabbi Elazar and Rabbi Aba rejoiced and said to him, "Come, you shall ride on the donkey and we shall walk along behind you."

But he told them, "Have I not told you that this is the command of the King, 'until the donkey driver appears.' This refers to *Mashiach*, who is described as 'poor and riding on a donkey.' "

They said to him: "You have not told us your name, or where you live."

He said: "Where I live is a good place and very precious to me. It is a very highly exalted tower that floats on air. And those who live in the tower are the Holy One, blessed be He, and one poor man. But I have been exiled from there, and came to drive the donkeys."

To Rabbi Elazar and Rabbi Aba, his words were sweet as honey. They said to him, "If you tell us the name of your father, we will kiss the earth under your feet."

He responded: "Why? It is not my habit to take pride in the study of the Torah. But the place where my father lives is in the Great Ocean, and he was a fish that swam from one end of the Great Ocean to the other. With his might, he was able to cross over the entire ocean in an instant, and he was able to swallow up all the other fish in the sea. Later he released them full of life and full of all the good in the world. And he released me, like an arrow from the hand of a valiant man, and hid me in the place of which I told you, the tower that floats on air, while he returned to his home in the ocean."

Rabbi Elazar thought about his words and said: "You are the son of the Light of the Torah. You are Rabbi Hamnunah Saba, the venerable! And you drive our donkeys for us!" Both Rabbi Elazar and Rabbi Aba wept and kissed him.

The rabbis have more than casual interest in the donkey driver's name. In the Zohar as well as in the Bible, names are linked not only to an individual's physical identity but also to his level of spiritual elevation. People's names tell us not only who they are in the world, but also where they are on the ascending path toward God. In this characteristically elliptical passage, the donkey driver reveals himself as a reincarnation of a great kabbalistic sage, whose name Hamnunah means *fish*. It should not surprise us that the driver refers to his former incarnation as his father. He is speaking in terms of spiritual lineage rather than biological genealogy.

They fell down on their faces in front of him. And as they fell, he disappeared. They rose and looked all around, but they could not see him, so they sat down and began to weep. At last Rabbi Aba said: "This is what we have learned. When righteous people go on a journey and occupy themselves with the study of Torah, they are visited by righteous souls from that other world, who reveal new explanations of the Torah. Surely this must be the reason Rabbi Hamnunah Saba came to us."

Then they got to their feet and tried to lead their donkeys, but the donkeys did not move. Fear struck them both, and they left the donkeys in their place. Even now, the site is called the "place of the donkeys."

As soon as the rabbis learn the identity of the donkey driver, he disappears! This can be understood as a set piece of magical storytelling, but a genuinely kabbalistic reading sees it in a much more up-to-date context. Werner Heisenberg, who formulated the so-called uncertainty principle of modern physics, taught that we cannot simultaneously know both the exact position and the exact velocity of a particle. In the act of observing one, we change the other. The uncertainty principle expresses both the power and the limits of perception in an extremely forceful way. Looking at something always changes it, according to Heisenberg, but because this change is continuous for as long as we look, we can never be certain of exactly what we see. Moreover, if that uncertainty is true for one observer, its effect is multiplied when there is more than one. If I myself can't be sure what is out there, even less can I rely on you to tell me. Like the child's game of telephone, the content of reality is always subject not just to change, but to severe distortion.

Like a subatomic particle whose location is subject to the uncertainty principle, the nature of the donkey driver changes when subjected to observation. Far from being contradicted by his lowly status in the world, his power and even his presence is at one with that circumstance. When his power is acknowledged and his status changes, he vanishes instantly. Kabbalah always identifies what is powerful with what is concealed, and this is especially true in its depiction of the great sages. Again and again beggars, harlots, and small children turn out to be prophets and angels.

Since everyone's mind is unique, how can anyone's description of reality be accepted? How can we place our trust in intermediaries even to tell us about the physical environment of our lives, let alone what is good for us? Yet this is what humanity has done for the past six thousand years, whether those intermediaries were shamans, priests, or natural scientists. There is no doubt that some good has come from this reliance on "experts," but most of the benefits have been on the physical level—and many of these have engendered new sets of problems. Spiritually, humanity's lot has hardly improved. Though many today would downplay that shortcoming, this is a serious lapse of judgment. Werner Heisenberg demonstrated that we must take all aspects of reality into account in order to grasp the totality of any object or event—yet we can never know all the aspects. Are we not, then, fundamentally "in the dark," however brightly lit the world might seem to be? If we have the courage to face facts, we must say good-bye to the security blanket that science has seemed to provide for us over the past several hundred years, just as we earlier said good-bye to witch doctors and conjurers. We must relinquish hope of finding the cause of chaos in the universe through observational means, and we must certainly abandon the idea of eradicating chaos with the same severely limited modalities.

This being the case, we must simply develop our spiritual potential in order to escape the chaos of a purely empirical relationship with the universe. All of this is implied in this remarkable section of the Zohar. So much is made clear in these few pages—but not too clear. The ultimate zoharic truth, of course, is that power derives from concealment, and that merit on the spiritual plane is linked to anonymity in the physical world. By the end of this story, therefore, we know that the donkey driver was a great kabbalist. He has spoken eloquently about *Shabbat*. But who was the donkey?

CHAPTER 5

THE LIGHT OF DESIRE

Vol. 3, pp. 15–16

Nothing is aroused above before it is aroused below.
Before the blue flame of the candle is aroused, it does
not hold the white flame. But as soon as the blue flame
is aroused, the white flame immediately rests upon it.

I t is so difficult to speak with certainty about Light. Light is
inherently mysterious. Though it enables us to see, Light
itself is invisible. When the beam of a flashlight shines
through darkness, we do not see the beam but only the objects it
strikes or the resistance it meets in the air. If we see color in the
Light, it is only the band of the spectrum that remains when the
others have been absorbed.

The Zohar has much to say about Light, and always in the context of paradox and mystery. Light is a central metaphor in Kabbalah, the symbol through which our relationship with the Creator
can be interpreted and understood. At the same time Light is not a
metaphor at all. It is the literal substance of the universe. It is the
raw material of the primordial Vessel whose remnants comprise all
reality, including our own bodies and our thoughts, hopes, and fears.

The Shattering of the Vessel is the defining kabbalistic event.
The Vessel shattered because of a contradiction in its nature, a ten-

sion between a desire to give and a desire to receive. The entire project of existence, even the creation of the universe itself, consists in resolving this duality through the unification of "getting" and "giving" into a single desire to "receive in order to share." When this is accomplished, Kabbalah teaches, the Vessel will at last be prepared to receive the Light of the Creator in full force.

The passage that opens this chapter uses the image of a candle flame as the source for a teaching on the power of desire, and on the relationship between the Upper and Lower Worlds. It is a precept of Kabbalah that our actions in the physical dimension create the channels that connect us to the Divine. In Greek and Roman mythologies, human beings are subject to fate and the will of the gods. But Kabbalah teaches that it is the marionettes who pull the strings. We ourselves initiate and perpetuate the Light's presence in our lives. Interactions between the physical and the supernal are always "ground-based."

When the Bible describes an angel appearing to an unsuspecting individual, or even the Creator Himself speaking to someone, this does not happen without an initial impetus arising from the world we live in. Thus, the Zohar asserts that the white light at the summit of a candle's flame cannot manifest without the foundation of the darker flame beneath it.

With this observation, the Zohar intends to illuminate one of the most important passages in the biblical narrative: the moment in which the Creator calls upon Abraham to leave his family circle and to strike out into the larger world.

Genesis 12:1–2

The Creator said to Abram, "Leave your country and your father's house, and go to a land that I will show you; and I will make you a great nation, and I will bless you, and make your name great."

Secular scholarship sees this as the end of the biblical creation story and the beginning of an epic that includes the travels of Abraham, the journey of Joseph into Egypt, the Exodus, and the entrance into the promised land. While the passage does represent an important transition, the Zohar finds its origin in a preceding biblical verse describing earlier doings by Abraham and his family:

Genesis 11:31–32

And Terah took Abram his son, and his grandson Lot the son of Haran, and Sarai his daughter-in-law, Abram's wife; and they went forth from Ur of the Chaldees to go into the land of Canaan, and they came to Haran and dwelt there.

As the Zohar interprets this:

And when they left to go to the land of Canaan, it was because they desired to go there. From this we learn that whoever asks to be purified will be helped. Come and behold this is so! The words "Go to the land of Canaan" are immediately followed by, "The Creator said to Abraham, 'Get you out!' " Before Abraham's desire to go was awakened, "Get you out" was not yet written.

The Bible introduces Abraham in the context of a long series of genealogies. Such passages strike many lay readers as irrelevant digressions. Perhaps for this very reason, the genealogies have been given careful attention by the kabbalistic sages. In this case, they are evidence of the Creator's long search for a soul worthy of becoming the forefather of His chosen people and the spiritual patriarch of all humanity. He at last found such a person in Abraham (called Abram until his circumcision in Genesis 17).

What exactly was so great about Abraham? He was seventy years old when he came to Haran, and another five years would pass before God spoke to him. What had he been doing all those years? How had he distinguished himself among all those carefully enumerated generations?

It is an axiom of Kabbalah that the Bible is an encrypted document—a code in which much is hidden and hinted at but little is explicitly revealed. Again and again the Zohar asserts the foolishness of a literal interpretation of the scriptures. We must read between the lines. We must extrapolate great truths from seemingly insignificant details. We must learn from the book's every word, just as in the world we must learn from every person. This is the task of the oral tradition and of Kabbalah's biblical commentaries on the Bible. These should not be understood as appendages to the Bible, but as revelations of what is hidden within it. Like an X ray of the text, they bring to light the underlying conditions from which the biblical narrative arises.

According to the oral tradition, the Creator tested Abraham ten times over the course of his lifetime. Four of those trials occurred before God ever spoke to him. Before Abraham's birth, for example, the tyrant Nimrod learned that a great leader was about to be born into the world. Nimrod ordained that all the firstborn sons in his kingdom should be put to death. But Abraham's father, Terah, was one of the ruler's most trusted ministers. At first Terah managed to avert the decree, but when this was no longer possible he hid the infant Abraham in a cave. He then turned over the child of one of his servants to the king's soldiers as if it had been his own.

Abraham, it is said, remained hidden in the cave for thirteen years—exactly the same fate that befell Rabbi Shimon bar Yochai when he went into hiding from the Romans. During his sequestration and later, when he found himself in the presence of his father's idols, Abraham applied himself to understanding the secrets of creation and the existence of the *Ein Sof,* the endless source of all Light. He undertook this task by three different means, which, taken together, represent all the basic modalities of spiritual search.

Abraham began with a logical critique of idol worship. How can anyone bow down to the sun, when it is obliterated by darkness at the end of every day? How can anyone worship the moon, when sunrise renders it invisible? Why should statues of wood or stone be held in awe, since even a child can smash them with a hammer or cast them down on the ground? At the same time as he was approaching the problem intellectually, Abraham felt in his heart that idol worship was an error and a sin. He had the gift of intuition, which has characterized the great investigators of the natural world, from the biblical personages to the quantum physicists. Last, Kabbalah teaches that Abraham in his youth had heard the truths of creation from Noah, whose father Lamech had been a contemporary of Adam himself. In the end, Abraham came away with an unshakable faith in God, and a profound understanding of the process by which He brought the universe into being. The first kabbalistic text, entitled *Sefer Yetzirah* (*The Book of Formation*), is said to have been composed by Abraham. In only a few thousand words, it describes creation in language that is at once obscure and wonderfully poetic.

As punishment for his refusal to embrace idol worship, Nimrod had Abraham thrown into a fiery furnace, but Abraham's faith saved him from death. It was then that Terah, although himself an idol worshipper, decided to flee with his family to the land of Canaan.

There is a clear similarity between the trials of Abraham and those inflicted on other characters later in the Bible. In fact, the trials are exactly the same. In the biblical book of Daniel, Shadrach, Meshach, and Abednego were also thrown into a fiery furnace for refusing to worship idols. The kabbalists would say that Abraham's fortitude opened a channel to courage for subsequent heroes facing similar circumstances—and not only for the heroes, but for us as well. Through the events of their lives and their exemplary responses to those events, the great biblical personages created a circuitry of energy to the Upper Worlds for use by future generations.

This is one of several important ideas in Kabbalah that would have been more difficult to explain before the inventions of the last hundred years or so. Today, fortunately, I can explain this difficult concept through a simple analogy from modern life. You may have noticed that the packaging of virtually every new product includes a toll-free, twenty-four-hour telephone number for getting help if problems arise. With everything from computers to toothpaste, you are only a phone call away from someone to talk you through your difficulty. In the same way, the biblical patriarchs and matriarchs created an all-inclusive directory of "access numbers" to an infinite variety of divine energies. If you are about to be thrown into a fiery furnace, through prayer or meditation you can tap into the energy channel created by Abraham under the same circumstances. More to the point, you can access that power whenever you are threatened with punishment or loss for your refusal to do something that you know is wrong.

Through all his trials, Abraham remained a pure being of *Chesed,* the divine emanation of kindness and mercy. He never wavered in his desire to serve God through service to his fellow human beings. Think of all the generations in which the Creator looked in vain for a human fit to become the patriarch of His nation. The unworthiness of those who were rejected lay not in their lack of righteousness, but in their lack of desire. Their desire to reveal the Light was not strong enough. The blue flame of the candle was insufficiently strong to cause the white flame to rest upon it.

Paradoxically, of course, the Creator knew all along that it would turn out this way. Just as He saw the whole future of hu-

manity at the time of creation, God saw Abraham and the greatness of his soul. Why, the sages asked, if Abraham was such an elevated being, was he not made the first human being, the one who
was entrusted with the Garden of Eden? Midrashic commentaries
suggest that the Creator decided to keep Abraham in reserve. If it
had been Abraham who succumbed to the temptation of the serpent, there would have been no one left to begin humanity's journey of redemption, which begins in Genesis 12.

Kabbalah presents Abraham as a man to whom nothing came
easily. Divine grace did not come to him in a flash, nor was he gifted
with sudden inspirations. But throughout his life he expressed the
essential quality of being to which we all must aspire: that is, the
desire to receive for the purpose of sharing. To ignite the blue flame
that the white flame may rest upon it, we, too, must cultivate the
wish to ignite the flame of our own being in order to bring Light to
others.

Therefore it is written, "Do not keep silent, Elohim,"
so that the white flame will never cease to exist in the
world—so that there will always be an awakening from
below upon which that from above will come to rest.

CHAPTER 6

THE THREE VISITORS: MERCY AND JUDGMENT

Modern physics describes four kinds of energy that animate the universe: the so-called strong force, that binds together the particles of the atomic nucleus; the weak force, that controls for the process of radioactive decay; gravity, or attraction inherent among particles of matter; and electromagnetism, the force derived from the presence, motion, and attraction of charged particles.

This last category provides an excellent analogy for Kabbalah's understanding of the spiritual circuitry of all Creation. Thousands of years before the discovery of electromagnetism by eighteenth-century scientists, the ancient kabbalists described the universe as permeated by spiritual forces endlessly circulating among three terminals, or "columns." The Right Column represents *Chesed*, or benevolence, mercy, and the desire to give and share. *Gvurah*— power, judgment, and the desire to receive—is expressed by the Left Column. The Central Column represents the mediating energy of choice and free will that enables us to meld and transform *Chesed* and *Gvurah* into a third form, which is desire to receive for the purpose of sharing. At all levels of our being, bringing about this transformation is nothing less than the genuine purpose of our lives.

Although Left-Column energy is often referred to as negative and Right-Column energy as positive, they are not really moral categories any more than one end of a flashlight battery is ethically superior to the other. All the energy forms are necessary for transformation to take place, just as an incandescent bulb needs both positive and negative poles, as well as the resistance of a central filament, to produce light.

The three energies are inherent to our nature, and interplay among the Right, Left, and Central Columns takes place at every moment. According to kabbalistic teaching, the "transmitters" from which those energies originate were the biblical patriarchs and matriarchs. This is an important and challenging concept, and one that deserves careful explanation. It requires not only an understanding of the individual characters of the Bible, but also insight into how they understood themselves and their mission in the world.

Kabbalah tells us that Abraham, Sarah, Isaac, Rebecca, Jacob, Rachel, Leah, and the other ancestral figures were real people. They were flesh and blood historical figures. They lived their lives in the physical world. They felt love, fear, hope, and disappointment. But they were also aware of their quite supernaturally important roles in creating the channels of energy that forever after would connect humanity to the Upper Worlds. These same channels connect us eternally to the patriarchs and matriarchs themselves, now that they have left the physical realm.

When Abraham, for example, performs certain actions or experiences certain emotions at specific points in the biblical narrative, the kabbalists explain that he is creating a channel to specific energies—a channel that, thanks to him, we can continue to use even today. It is as if a permanently open telephone connection were brought into being, linking us to certain aspects of the Creator's Light. Through this connection, we can bring the divine presence into our physical environment. In Hebrew, this presence is referred to as the Shechinah. It is the immanent form of the Divine, and it is traditionally understood to be of a female nature.

A conventional interpretation of the book of Genesis might point to Abraham as an example of a righteous man, which he surely was. But Kabbalah emphasizes Abraham's role as an architect of the spiritual system: that is, as one of the builders of the spiritual circuitry linking us to the Upper Worlds. We can use this circuitry to illuminate not only our thoughts, prayers, and meditations, but even our most routine everyday activities.

If we were to create an overall image of the kabbalistic universe, the Upper and Lower Worlds could be compared to a tree, in which the continuous interaction between the root system and the branches manifest the fundamental teaching, "As above, so below." Although the two aspects of this metaphorical tree are not visible to each other, the flow of energy between them expresses the principles of both metaphysical and physical realms. The issue of how we can achieve certainty, therefore, is addressed by Kabbalah through a principle of correspondence. The physical world has been patterned on the world above. By reflecting wisely on the material realm, we can glimpse the supernal dimension.

By referring to Kabbalah as a spiritual circuitry, whether electrical or arboreal, the intention is to emphasize the flowing quality of the Creator's Light—the paths through which it can be channeled, just as electricity can be drawn through a cable or water through the roots, branches, and leaves of a growing plant.

The eighteenth chapter of Genesis, along with the Zohar's commentaries, provide an excellent example of these principles in action. Abraham is now one hundred years old. God has recently promised him that he will be the father of a great nation, and this covenant has been formalized by Abraham's circumcision. Yet the old man whose progeny "will outnumber the stars in the sky" does not yet have even one child! When God told Abraham what the future holds (in Genesis 17) Abraham literally fell down laughing!

Genesis 18:1–5

By the oak trees of Mamre, the Creator appeared to Abraham; he was sitting at the entrance of the tent as the day grew hot. Looking up, he saw three men standing near him. As soon as he saw them, he ran from the entrance of the tent to greet them and, bowing to the ground, he said, "My lords, if it please you, do not go past your servant. Let a little water be brought; bathe your feet and recline under the tree. And let me fetch a morsel of bread that you may refresh yourselves; then go on, seeing that you have come your servant's way." They replied, "Do as you have said."

As the narrative opens, it has been three days since the circumcision. Although God commanded him to undergo the rite, the oral tradition tells us that Abraham did not immediately comply. Despite the commonplace impression of the Old Testament God as a stern and demanding monarch, Abraham's relationship with the Creator extends to him much more freedom of choice than we might expect. There is a surprising level of give-and-take in their interactions, and divine commands are often negotiated rather than merely obeyed.

Regarding his circumcision, a midrash describes how Abraham consulted three friends before deciding to go ahead. According to one version of the story, all three friends told him to avoid circumcision. Yet this is exactly why he decided to undergo it. As happens several times in the narrative of his life, Abraham saw what others didn't see. Kabbalah teaches that the truth is almost never what it seems. Abraham, the first kabbalist, knew that the correct path can be revealed by the disapproval of others.

The third day after circumcision is the most painful. This is when the Creator chose to visit Abraham, at least in part to comfort him. Interpretations of Genesis 18 most often focus on the annunciation of Sarah's forthcoming pregnancy. But the theme of solicitude and sensitivity to the needs of others is equally present, and there is certainly no doubt that Abraham is feeling exquisitely sensitive himself, both physically and spiritually. And in terms of the spiritual circuitry discussed earlier, we should understand God's visit as opening the channel of sympathy for those in pain and identifying sympathy as a divine attribute.

The Torah's description refers to the heat of the day, an external representation of Abraham's pain. The heat also suggests the spiritual process that is under way, as if the day itself were a crucible of transformation. And heat also provides an occasion for revealing Abraham's qualities of mercy, solicitude, and generosity, as befits his identification with *Chesed,* the Right-Column energy. Abraham is seated at the entrance of his tent to welcome travelers who may need his help on this torrid day, a day so hot that a hole to hell is said to have been opened in the ground. God intentionally made the day oppressively hot so there would not be any travelers for Abraham to take care of. Yet Abraham's nature is to give and share. He is literally not himself unless he is doing so. According to the oral tradition, he sent his servant out into the desert to look for travelers, and when none were found, he went out to look himself!

Finally, when he was sitting in the entrance of his tent, the Creator appeared to him. But how did this appearance take place? Did God appear in front of him, or above him, or to one side of him? The text seems ambiguous, at least when read as literal description.

The kabbalists suggest that Abraham had been looking downward when God appeared, since the next sentence says he "looked up" and saw three human forms. He was looking down into himself, into his own soul, and this is where the Creator appeared. Then he looked up and the three beings were before him.

Vol. 3, pp. 271–273

> The words "appeared to him" mean that the Shechinah appeared to him through those grades that are attached to Her own aspects, referring to Michael on the right side, Gabriel on the left side, Rafael to the front. . . . The Shechinah appeared to him among the oak trees—the shadows of the world—to show them the first circumcision, the Holy Imprint according to the secret of the Faith in the whole world.

Immediately Abraham knows these are not ordinary people. After all, he has already determined that the roads are empty of travelers on this overheated day. They are three individual angels, and collectively they are the Shechinah, the aspect of the Creator that manifests itself in the world. Spiritual reality, the Zohar tells us, can choose to reveal itself in material form. Thus disguised, spiritual energies may take part in the physical world. "Nor could the world bear to co-exist with them if they were not thus clothed," the Zohar further explains. The intensity of their presence would be too much for us to bear.

But how can we know when this is the case? How can we be certain that it is not an angel behind the wheel of our taxicab or operating the cash register at our supermarket? The Zohar assures us that we cannot be certain. Therefore we are well advised to treat everyone as an emissary of the Divine, with Abraham as a model for this.

These three emissaries have come for very specific reasons.

> Rafael, who governs the power to heal, helped Abraham recover from the circumcision. Michael came to inform Sarah that she shall bear a son . . .

As always, Abraham's instinct is to be of service, but now he puts himself out even more than usual. Why does he do so? The identity of the third angel offers a clue.

> And Gabriel, who came to overturn Sodom . . . is responsible for all the Judgments in the world.

Whenever a judgment has been rendered in the Upper Worlds, there is always a chance to moderate the judgment—to "sweeten" it, in the traditional phrasing—through the performance of some worthy action.

Vol. 3, p. 322

When the Creator loves a person, He sends him a present. And what is that present? It is a poor man for whom he can perform a meritorious act. . . .

Come and behold: when the Creator planned to execute Judgment on Sodom, He prepared a meritorious act for Abraham by sending him a present, which refers to the three angels. . . .

When harsh Judgment hangs over the world, the Holy One remembers the charitable deeds that men performed. Every time a person performs a meritorious action, it is noted above. As it is written, "charity delivers from death." (Proverbs 11:4) According to this, the Holy One arranged in advance that opportunity for Abraham to perform a meritorious action. . . .

Abraham's behavior suggests that he was well aware of this chance to ameliorate a harsh judgment. In our own lives, however, we may be less attentive to such opportunities. They always come well disguised—nothing dramatic or obviously important. It is simply an occasion for performing a small charitable act, something seemingly unconnected to any larger circumstance. But Kabbalah teaches that righteousness cannot be measured as large or small. Indeed, it is a kabbalistic principle that the greatest power resides in whatever seems small and insignificant.

Abraham did not need to rely on his intuition to discern the importance of these visitors. A tree beside his tent bloomed or withered according to the spiritual elevation of whomever stood beneath it, and the midrash reports that the tree abruptly blossomed in the presence of the three strangers!

As the Zohar specifies, each of these personages had come for a specific purpose: Raphael to heal Abraham's wound, Michael to confirm God's promise of Abraham as the founder of a great people, and Gabriel to destroy the cities of Sodom and Gomorrah. All these purposes are related, and all bear on the theme of mercy or solicitude. Abraham's awareness of a pending judgment against the two cities of the plain was also a factor in his interaction with the strangers. His nephew Lot was living in Sodom, and it was not long before Abraham found himself bargaining with the Creator to spare Lot's life when the city was destroyed. To the extent that he was successful, it was because of the merit he had acquired through his generosity to the three strangers. In Kabbalah, righteous action is never just a matter of sympathy or altruism. Doing good is in our own self-interest. Doing good brings us strength. In addition to hastening the transformation of our souls, righteous action gives us practical power to make our most important wishes come true, and to prevent our worst fears from being realized.

Abraham offers the visitors food, and they accept. In fact, they eat before speaking, lest Abraham think they speak in order to obtain food. But angels are not corporeal beings. They do not eat. A celestial flame consumed the meal provided by Abraham, though he saw nothing of this.

Then occurs one of the most enigmatic moments in all the scriptures.

Genesis 18:9

They said to him, "Where is your wife Sarah?" And he replied, "There, in the tent." Then one said, "I will return to you when life is due, and your wife Sarah shall have a son!" Sarah was listening at the entrance of the tent, which was behind him. Now Abraham and Sarah were old, advanced in years; Sarah had stopped having the periods of women. And Sarah laughed to herself, saying, "Now that I am withered, am I to have enjoyment—with my husband so old?"

Was the message concerning Isaac's birth intended for Sarah, and not for Abraham, who after all had heard it earlier from God? Midrashic commentaries assert that Sarah's listening to a conversation not intended for her caused her to misconstrue its meaning, and to laugh when laughter was uncalled for. Still other commentaries interpret Sarah's laughter more positively: She laughed with surprise and joy, for at that moment her menstrual blood flowed at the age of ninety-seven. In any case, the Creator questioned Sarah's laughter, and her doubt that the angel's promise would come to pass.

Genesis 18:13–15

Then the Creator said to Abraham, "Why did Sarah laugh, saying, 'shall I in truth bear a child, old as I am?' Is anything too wondrous for the Creator? I will return to you at the time that life is due, and Sarah shall have a son."

From a kabbalistic perspective, this passage concerning the promise to Sarah exemplifies the principle of the general being contained within the particular, and the macrocosm in the microcosm. Just as the Creator restored Sarah's womb, so does he also lead us toward our own transformation and unity with Him.

CHAPTER 7

STRANGERS:
"THINK WELL OF EVERYONE"

Our purpose in life is spiritual transformation, and every encounter with a stranger is an opportunity to draw closer to that purpose. Every human being is a universe, and, like all universes, every person is still in the process of creation. When we come into someone's life, we enter an alternate world, and by entering it we change it. This is much more than just a philosophical concept or the premise for a science fiction novel. Right now, there are almost certainly hundreds of people within a few miles of you, and more likely there are thousands. Most of these people have no idea that you exist, yet each of them comprises an entire universe, just as you do. Each of them carries all of creation in their hearts and minds. When you cross paths with a stranger, a dimension comes into being, one in which *both* of you reside. Every interaction with a new person is an opportunity to transform both your life and theirs. This is an immense opportunity, if only we choose to recognize and take advantage of it. Every encounter with a stranger is a chance to start over.

But we rarely see "ordinary" experiences from this perspective. Too often in the modern world encounters with strangers are burdened by negative expectations or bored indifference. It should not be surprising, therefore, given the importance that Kabbalah ascribes to these encounters, that the Zohar deals with them very explicitly, as in the paragraphs that follow.

Vol. 6, pp. 267–269

Rabbi Chiya and Rabbi Yosi were walking when they saw an armed man wearing a prayer shawl. Rabbi Chiya said: "Perhaps this man is very pious, or perhaps he is some very dangerous person in disguise." Rabbi Yosi replied: "The righteous have said to judge all persons favorably. We have learned that when a man sets out on a journey, he should be prepared for three courses of action: to give gifts, to fight, and to pray. We know this from Jacob, who prepared himself for these three things. We see that this man is wearing a prayer shawl, which shows that he is ready to pray, and he is also carrying a weapon, so he is prepared to fight. If he has these two, he must have the third."

This passage calls to mind Exodus 13:18, "And the people of Israel were well-armed when they left Egypt." Concerning the meaning of "well-armed," the great sage Rabbi Yaakov Yitzchak Horowitz (1745–1815) wrote, "What were their weapons? Only the many miracles that had already taken place. For when a miracle occurs, a channel is opened and never closed, so that the power of the miracle can easily be called upon forever thereafter. The miracle of their escape from bondage was the people's sword when they left Egypt, and the sword of that miracle would serve them throughout the ages."

But when they greeted the traveler, he did not respond. Rabbi Chiya said: "It seems that he lacks one of the requirements of a journey. He is not prepared to offer

gifts, which includes the exchange of greetings." Rabbi
Yosi replied: "Perhaps he is praying, or perhaps he is
concentrating on his studies."

Humor in the literature of the past is a perishable commodity,
especially in ancient texts to which we reflexively ascribe high seri-
ousness. But this is no doubt intended to be a funny situation,
which becomes clear if we transpose it to a contemporary setting:

Two friends are walking down the street when they see a man
dressed like a Chasid, but with a machine gun hidden under his
coat. "There is a man who's either a rabbi or a bank robber," says one
of the friends. "Well," says the other, "let's try to look positively at
this. . . ."

Even without introducing weapons hidden under prayer shawls,
we should understand that the Zohar is referring to circumstances
in which we are predisposed toward dislike or suspicion of another
human being. Once again placing this in a modern context, it could
be a person in a supermarket checkout line who has two hundred
coupons to redeem. It could be a driver who cuts in and out of traf-
fic. Or, if you are feeling sufficiently out of sorts, it could be any-
body.

But the fact that anger toward strangers is a common situation,
or even one that sometimes has humorous overtones, does not diminish its spiritual significance. On the contrary, a teaching such as
"judge all persons favorably" erases the distinction between the
mundane and the profoundly metaphysical. In Kabbalah, what we
do in this world always has effects in the spiritual dimension. Negative behavior foments chaos in the Upper Worlds, and this sets
back the progress of all humanity toward oneness with God. It is
important to realize that there is no relativity of scale in this. As in
scientific theories of turbulence and complexity, a small disturbance
in our relations with other people is amplified through the dimen-

sions of being. The importance that Kabbalah attaches to this principle cannot be overemphasized. Thus, the sages tell us that causing embarrassment to any person is the equivalent of murder!

In this instance the rabbis behave in an exemplary manner, and their forbearance is rewarded:

> They continued on, yet the man in the prayer shawl remained silent. Finally Rabbi Chiya and Rabbi Yosi began a discussion of Torah between themselves. As soon as their fellow traveler heard this he drew nigh and gave the two friends greetings of peace. He asked: "What were your thoughts when you offered me greeting but I did not answer?" Rabbi Yosi answered: "I thought perhaps you were engaged in prayer or studies." The man replied: "As you judged me favorably, may the Creator judge you likewise. Let me explain my actions to you. One day on the road I encountered a man and greeted him in peace. The man turned out to be a robber. He attacked me and I was forced to defend myself. Had I not overcome him, I would have been badly hurt. Since that day, I vowed to greet only a man whom I knew to be righteous. Moreover, it is forbidden to greet an evil man, as it is written, 'There is no peace for the wicked.' (Isaiah 48:22)
>
> "When I saw you and you greeted me, I did not respond, for I suspected you were not righteous, because I did not see any prayer shawls on you. Besides, I was indeed concentrating on my studies. But now that I know that you are righteous men, the way is clear before me." He then began to discourse on the verse, "The Creator is good to Israel, to such as are of a clean heart." (Psalms 73:1)

He said: "For governing the world, the Creator made a Right and a Left. One is called good and the other is called evil. Man includes them both. The idolatrous nations are included within evil, the Left, which was created for the defilement of their side, as they are uncircumcised of heart and in their flesh. But of Israel it is written, 'Truly God is good to Israel.'

"You may say He is good to all of Israel, but that is not true. He is good only to those who were not defiled with evil, as it is written, 'To such as are of a clean heart.' He is good to Israel so that they cleave to the supreme mystery, in the secret of faith, so that all shall become one."

Rabbi Yosi said: "We are happy not to have mistaken you, for you were sent to us by the Creator." He continued: "Since good is meant for Israel, Israel will have a portion in this world and also in the world to come, to see the sight of glory eye to eye. It is written, 'For they shall see, eye to eye, the Creator returning to Zion.' " (Isaiah 52:8)

There are phrases in these final paragraphs that may seem disturbing in a modern context: the reference, for example, to "idolatrous nations . . . uncircumcised of heart and in their flesh" who are thus "defiled." We should be aware that "nations" does not denote a political or ethnic identity. It refers to a spiritual category of people— or, rather, people who are without spirituality, who worship the idols of the material world. In the same way, "circumcision" does not refer to a medical procedure. Kabbalistically, circumcision refers to the sacred and everlasting covenant between humanity and the Creator described in Genesis 17, of which Abraham's circumcision was the sign and symbol. Those who choose the negative path, whether in action or in thought, exclude themselves from the sacred covenant and are said to be "uncircumcised in their flesh and in their hearts."

"You shall not wrong a stranger or oppress him, for you were strangers in the land of Egypt" (Exodus 22:18) is a teaching repeated many times in the Bible and its commentaries. And the Zohar puts it even more strongly: "Judge all persons favorably." We must not set ourselves against those who have not advanced along their spiritual path as far as we have. As this selection indicates, they may have traveled further than we imagine.

CHAPTER 8

THE UNNAMEABLE: CHAOS

There are two female presences in the opening chapters of the Bible. One of course, is Eve, "the mother of all the living." Another female is there also, although the Zohar refers to her as without gender, lurking between the lines of text even as the kabbalists teach that she hides in shadows and unlit doorways. Beyond the book of Genesis, this same extremely negative—in fact, demonic—entity appears several times in the Bible. Usually she is "disguised" as another character—it is she and her equally evil sister who appear before King Solomon as two harlots arguing over possession of a baby. The power of this negative entity is taken very seriously in Kabbalah. We must guard against her influence at all times. We are not to speak or write her name. Yet she does appear in the Scriptures, in the book of Isaiah 34:14, though in some translations "night hag" or "screech owl" is substituted for her forbidden name.

And the Zohar, of course, never refers to her by name. She is called the Klipah (Heb. *shell*), which also denotes a kind of husk that can form around us when we succumb to negative or self-serving influences. Yet Kabbalah does not describe the Klipah as utterly alien to the Creator's Light. She is composed of *degraded* Light, *fallen* Light, *corroded* Light. The Klipah is like a powerful battery that has lain for many years on the ocean floor, which, as the

Zohar explains, is exactly where this vile and dangerous female was relegated to spend a great deal of time. As with most biblical characters, the Klipah is understood both as metaphor and a physical entity. In the biblical text, she can be construed as a personification of corrupt aggressive or sexual feelings. But she is also depicted as a very malignant reality of our lives.

The Zohar tells us that the Klipah came into being on the fifth day of creation, as described in Genesis 1:21. She is identified with the "great sea monsters" mentioned in that verse, and with the multitudes of creeping beings that the sea brought forth. Immediately after her creation, the Klipah flew toward heaven, where she found herself attracted to the sparks of divine Light that surround the Creator. These sparks are the "small faces" in the following Zohar passage. They can be thought of as angels, of which Kabbalah describes several types. The lowest category of angel is simply a flicker of energy that localizes in a particular form, sometimes for only a moment. The Klipah attached herself to these beings, until God forced her to descend to Eden, where Adam and Eve had been created. Drawn to Adam's beauty, the Klipah desired union with him, but realized also that she could not distract him from the splendor of Eve, whose beauty was one with that of heaven itself. The Klipah then returned to the Upper World, tried once again to conjoin with the angels, but soon found herself cast by God into the sea from which she had first emerged. The Zohar describes these events:

Vol. 1, pp. 286–287

When the Klipah saw Eve clinging to the side of Adam, who represented the beauty of above, and saw in them the complete form, she flew up from her place

and wanted to cling to the small faces of Adam and
Eve as before. However, the guards at the gates did not
allow this. The Creator scolded the Klipah and cast her
into the depths of the sea.

The Klipah is associated with what is "covered up" or shrouded
in murkiness. Concealment often has positive connotations in Kabbalah, when its purpose is to reveal the Light of God. But this hiding in the shadows is decidedly negative. It is based in shame, and
its intention is to avoid the consequences of prior action. As the
Zohar recounts, the Klipah remained in the sea until the sin of
Adam and Eve.

Then the Creator removed the Klipah from the depths
of the sea. The Klipah took power over all those
children—the "small faces" of mankind—who deserve
punishment for the sins of their fathers.

The Klipah's diabolically negative energy is drawn to children—
the "angels" of the world—just as it was attracted to the true angels
in the Upper World. This is consistent with the teaching that children are in a sense closer to God than other human beings. Their
souls were more recently in the Upper World.

Notice how the Zohar is unconstrained by conventional ideas of
linear time. If Adam and Eve had just fallen, how could the Klipah
already be making raids on the progeny of future generations? This
is not a "mistake," but a characteristic of prophetic narratives. Just
as perspective did not appear in the graphic arts until the Renais-
sance, continuity of time is not an imperative in kabbalistic texts.
There is a clear intention to subvert or even violate the demands of
realism. Like modern physics, Kabbalah teaches that the past has

already occurred but is also still occurring. As shards of the one primordial soul, we have already done things that, as individuals, we
are continually reprising. In Kabbalah, once something has happened it keeps happening forever, or at least until the final transformation and the return to Paradise.

Returning from its depredations across space and time, the
Klipah made her way to the gates of Eden, where she rested beside
the flaming sword described in Genesis. This sword can be likened
to the scale of Zeus in Greek myth. It manifests mercy or judgment
alternately. And when judgment is expressed, the Klipah returns
to the physical realm.

> The Klipah wandered around the world, approached
> the gates of the Garden of Eden, and sat down
> near the blade of the sword, for it was the flame of the
> sword that the Klipah had originated. When the bright
> blade of the sword revolved and changed to judgment,
> the Klipah fled. She roams the world and finds chil-
> dren deserving of punishment. The Klipah laughs with
> the children and then kills them.

Again moving from the past to the future, and then back into
the past, the Zohar mentions the Klipah's intercourse with Cain
(Kayin). As usual, she is rejected or frustrated in her first attempt at
connection, but she persists with evil energy. Many of the negative
forces loose in the world are the offspring of Cain and the Klipah.

> When Kayin was born, the Klipah was unable to cleave
> to him, but later she approached him, cleaved to him,
> and manifested to him earthbound spirits and flying
> spirits.

While these teachings may seem quite remote from our everyday experience, the history of Adam after the Fall has definite lessons for contemporary life. When he realizes the terrible consequences of his actions at the Tree of Knowledge of Good and Evil, the Zohar describes Adam's descent into what might today be called a state of depression, in the sense that depression is disconnection from the Light.

> Adam had intercourse with the female spirits for 130 years, until Naamah came. Because of her beauty, she led the sons of Elohim, Aza, and Azael astray. She bore them all sorts of new Klipot. Evil spirits and demons spread out from her into the world. They wander around during the night. Whenever they find men sleeping alone in their own homes, they hover over them and cling to them, arousing lustful desires and having offspring by them.

In a sense, Adam fell into the same trap twice. His first bite of the forbidden fruit was not the real cause of the trouble. It was the reactive second bite that really manifested desire to receive for himself alone. And now, despondent over his interpretation of the past, he believed himself beyond all redemption.

Who has not, at one time or another, succumbed to this same kind of thinking? Who has not fallen victim to this extremely potent weapon of the negative side? Kabbalah teaches that this voluptuous acceptance of defeat is really a kind of egomania in reverse. We convince ourselves that our failures exist on such a grand scale that not even the Creator can deliver us from them. But it is really self-importance that makes this self-pity possible.

It is critical that we remain aware of the existence of the Klipah and practice spiritual discernment in our active pursuit of the Light. While desire is requisite to draw Light to ourselves, desire can be implemented in negative ways. With what prescience the Zohar anticipates the psychology of addiction. An addict, whether of drugs, alcohol, gambling, or sex, is understood by contemporary psychotherapy as a *failed* seeker after true joy. An addict is a person with strong needs and desires—which is all to the good, Kabbalah would say—but out of this strong need comes an impatience to satisfy it quickly and intensely—and then, because the intensity fades, to satisfy it again and again. *Satisfy*, however, is not really the right word. Addiction really palliates genuine fulfillment. It is a desire for the Light that is pursued in the wrong way.

CHAPTER 9

THE SHECHINAH:
GOD IN THE WORLD

I n biblical times, the Creator's presence was not only experienced in people's hearts and minds, but was also available to the senses. Although God could not be seen directly, He was visibly manifest in such forms as a cloud or a pillar of fire, and also His voice could be heard—if not by everyone, at least by patriarchs such as Abraham and Moses. Gradually, however, the Creator became less tangible and localized. In contradistinction to the wood and stone images of idol worshippers, the sages tell us that the essence of God lies not only beyond reach of our senses, but also beyond our intellectual powers. Many realms of being now separate us from the Creator. Though it is our task through our spiritual work to traverse those realms and ultimately to become one with the divine, in our everyday lives we must experience God indirectly—through the emanations of His Light, and through the divine presence that Kabbalah identifies as the Shechinah.

Shechinah is derived from the Hebrew verb *shakhan*, meaning "to dwell" or "to dwell within." Significantly, because gender is ascribed to verbs in Hebrew, the feminine nature of the Shechinah is evident in the word itself. The Shechinah is the female aspect of the Light. It is the energy of manifestation, and as such it is the expression of the Light that is closest to our physical realm. In his authoritative study of ancient religion entitled *The Hebrew Goddess*, the late anthropologist Raphael Patai traced the historical development of the Shechinah among the people of Israel. Patai was a scholarly rather than a spiritual writer, but within the limits of an academic perspective he clearly delineates the Shechinah's growing importance in the spiritual life of ancient Israel, especially as the view of the Creator became more abstract. According to Patai, the Shechinah evolved a clear identity as the aspect of God that is present in our world and that can be perceived by the senses of those who are spiritually attuned. As such, she is an important antidote to other, readily available but negative versions of spirituality, including idol worship, and a susceptibility to the Angel of Darkness, who is continuously "roaming all over the earth." (Job 1:7) The Shechinah has a distinctly female energy and individuality.

Although the explications offered by Patai and other scholars are interesting, we should not let them distract us from understanding Kabbalah as far more than a historical phenomenon. The Zohar is not just a cultural artifact—and, most important, the Shechinah is a genuine presence in our lives, as these paragraphs from the Zohar illustrate.

Vol. 2, pp. 163–169

Rabbi Shimon was traveling to Tiberias, accompanied by Rabbi Yosi, Rabbi Yehuda, and Rabbi Chiya. On the way, they saw Rabbi Pinchas coming toward them. When they met Rabbi Pinchas, everyone dismounted and sat under one of the trees on the mountain. Rabbi Pinchas said, "Now that we are seated, I would like to hear some of the good teachings that you expound every day."

Rabbi Shimon then opened a discourse by saying, " 'And he [Abraham] went on his journeys from the

Negev' (Genesis 13:3). Why does the scripture say 'journeys' rather than 'journey'? Because there were two journeys, one of Abraham, and the second that of the Shechinah. This dual journey indicates that everyone should be both male and female, so that our faith may be strong and the Shechinah may never depart from us."

When the kabbalists speak of our dual nature as both male and female, this does not refer to gender-based characteristics in the ordinary sense. Rather, the reference is to a balance of giving and receiving energies. Just as an electrical circuit requires positive and negative poles, both energies are necessary to create a complete spiritual circuitry. Once his desire had drawn to Abraham the Creator's order to go forth from his father's, Abraham drew the divine feminine presence into himself, and thereby created an internal balance that protected him against negative influences. The Zohar asserts that each of us should do the same and explains exactly what this involves.

When a man is at home, the foundation of the house is the wife, because of whom the Shechinah does not leave the house. He who goes on a journey should pray to the Creator before departing, so as to draw the Shechinah upon himself. And when through his prayers the Shechinah rests upon him, then he can go on his way. When the Shechinah rests upon him, he can be male and female both in the city and in the field—that is, in his home and on his journey.

As long as a man is traveling, he should beware of sinning, so that the Shechinah will not desert him and cause him to become defective—that is, not composed of male and female. Just as he guards his actions in the city, when his wife is with him, he should do so all the more on the road, when his supernal mate, the Shechinah, is attached to him.

When he returns home, he should please his wife, for it is she who procured the supernal mate for him. And when he comes to her, he should please her for two reasons. First, because of the joy of mating, which is the joy of fulfilling a precept, and our rejoicing in a precept is the joy of the Shechinah.

The great scholars abstain from their wives all weekdays, so as not to be distracted from their full occupation with the Torah. The supernal mate, the Shechinah, consorts with them, and does not leave them, so that they remain male and female. And when *Shabbat* comes, these scholars have to please their wives for the honor of the supernal mate, as we have explained.

And if he does not mate with his wife, is that a sin? Evidently so, for he has diminished the glory of his supernal mate, who has mated with him on the way because of the actions of his wife.

There is a second reason why he should gladden his wife. By his mating with his wife, he causes the mating of the Creator with the Shechinah. If a man's wife conceives in consequence of this mating, the supernal mating endows her with a holy soul. It behooves one, therefore, to concentrate on that joy, as one should concentrate on mating on *Shabbat*. That is, the holiness of mating when one returns from a journey equals the holiness of the mating on the eve of *Shabbat*.

Hence the quotation "You shall know that your tent is at peace" indicates that you will know the Shechinah is with you and has settled on your home. Further, "and you shall visit your habitation and not sin" means that you should not sin by refraining from intercourse before the Shechinah, which is the joy in fulfilling a precept. One must not prevent the union of the Creator with the Shechinah, through which a soul can be endowed. This is a great sin.

These are very challenging passages, so let us begin a discussion of them with a brief summary of exactly what is being said. When a man is at home, the Zohar says, he should maintain good relations with his wife. In this way he creates the balanced, harmonious, and altogether complete environment in which the divine presence—the Shechinah—can comfortably reside. There may come a time, however, in which such a man must leave his home to embark on a journey, perhaps a long one. Kabbalist Rabbi Akiva, for example, was away from his wife for twenty-four years.

While he is on the road, how can he maintain the balance of male and female principles that protects him against the evil inclination and connects him to the Upper Worlds? It is the Shechinah that enables him to do this. Because he propitiated the Shechinah when he was at home, she now accompanies him when he is away. She becomes his wife, in the sense that she enables him to balance the energies of giving and receiving, and to maintain the stability of his inner self. When a man returns home, it is his responsibility to resume positive relations with his wife—emotionally, spiritually, and especially sexually.

The Zohar emphasizes the importance of treating one's wife with the utmost love, honor, and respect. A man must make every attempt to elevate his wife to the highest level. In pursuing their own goals, even spiritual ones, some men relegate their wives to a secondary role. But a man can never find spiritual fulfillment without elevating his wife to her rightful place.

> And upon this, we commented, "And he came onto the place and he slept there" (Genesis 28:11), meaning that he asked permission first. From this we learn that he who wants to mate with his wife must soothe her first and soften her with sweet talk. Failing to do so, he shall not sleep with her, because their desire must be mutual and without coercion.
>
> Loving words, spoken to win a woman's affections, draw her closer to him, and arouse love within her. See how tender and how love-enticing are the words, "A bone of my bones and flesh of my flesh." (Genesis 2:23) They show her that the two are one and inseparable. And then he should praise her, saying, "This one shall be called woman," which means she is peerless and the pride of the house. Other women, compared to her, are as apes before men. "This one shall be called woman," perfect in every regard, she and no other. All those are loving words, similar to those in the verse, "Many girls have done great things, but you have excelled them all."

The Zohar presents several reasons for its frank celebration of sex in marriage, beyond the inherent pleasure in mating referred to in the third paragraph just cited. First, good marital relations fulfills a divine precept. This in itself always brings joy, both to those who fulfill the precept and to the Shechinah. The Zohar also suggests that in the absence of physical contact between man and wife, the Shechinah will feel unrecognized for the spiritual sustenance she provided during the husband's journey.

Moreover, the earthly mating brings about a connection in the Upper Worlds between the Creator and the Shechinah herself, who is at the same time an aspect of God and also His consort. Through these conjugal relations on different levels of being, a soul can be born into the world—and perhaps a great soul, owing to the especially positive energy available when sex is resumed after a journey.

This is what the Zohar explicitly says. Access to its full meaning requires us to approach this chapter in a fundamentally different way than we would read a newspaper or work of nonfiction. The Zohar is unconstrained by everyday demarcations between individual characterizations and wide-ranging allegories. The story of one person can effortlessly turn into the story of all people. An incident that seems to occur in a moment can take place across the true limitlessness of time. When the Zohar speaks of a man going on a journey, therefore, we must immediately be aware of the macrocosm in the microcosm. Every journey is a spiritual one, most especially the journey of life itself.

According to kabbalistic teaching, if we are fortunate enough to grow up in a home in which the male and female principles are in balance, we can remain connected to that balance as we negotiate the circuitous path from childhood to maturity. This is the real journey that the Zohar is considering. At its conclusion, as we establish a new home in adulthood, we can re-create for our own children the strong foundation that was of such benefit to us. In this interpretation, the Zohar is discussing not just the principles of a strong marriage in an individual life but the paradigm of emotional development throughout lifetime, and even across generations. And that is by no means the end. The Zohar tells us that by creating an ambiance of domestic bliss in our earthly homes, we inspire God to do the same above. We literally re-create the moment of creation.

This both fortifies and reverses the Freudian schema of psychosexual development, according to which a man must come not only to accept but to identify with what first seems unimaginable: the intimate relations between his father and mother. Now, much more than just reenacting those relations, we can actually ignite them in the Upper Worlds. Not only can we do this, but we must do it, for the sake of the souls who are eagerly waiting to be born.

On the subject of marriage and children, the Zohar is straightforward and adamant: To complete our spiritual correction in this lifetime, we should marry and raise a family. The energies of giving and receiving are not properly balanced outside marriage, and an out-of-balance soul is a soul infinitely more vulnerable to chaos. The issue of children is treated even more emphatically, for here there is not just one soul at stake, but many others that need to enter the world. Whoever remains childless denies them this opportunity. This is a turning away from Kabbalah's most basic teaching of how we should live in the world. At the most fundamental level, it is a refusal to become a sharing human being.

The Zohar makes this point through the story of King Hezikiah, from the book of Isaiah:

Vol. 7, pp. 200–203

Rabbi Yehuda opened the discussion with the verse "Then Hezikiah turned his face toward the wall, and prayed to the Creator." (Isaiah 38:2) Why is Hezikiah different from others who prayed, of whom it does not say that they turned their faces to the wall, but of whom it suffices to say that they "prayed to the Creator"? For whoever prays may do so with proper intention, even if he does not turn his face to the wall, as it is written of Moses, "And Moses prayed to the Creator."

The secret of the matter is what we learned of Hezikiah: that he was not married at the time. He had no wife, nor did he beget any children. It is therefore written, "And Isaiah came to him, and said to him 'For you shall die, and you shall not live.' " (Isaiah 38:1) This means "you shall die" in this world, "and you shall not live" in the world to come. Why? Because Hezikiah had no wife, and did not beget children.

Whoever does not strive to beget children in this world has no existence in the world to come, nor any portion thereof. His soul is driven from the world, and cannot find rest in any place. This is the punishment indicted in the Torah by the words: "They shall die childless." (Exodus 20:20)

Moreover, the Shechinah did not rest upon him at all. From the words: "Then Hezikiah turned his face toward the wall," we understand that he had decided to take a wife, so that the Shechinah, the secret of the wall, would rest upon him.

Here the Zohar identifies the Shechinah with a wall—an association with the Ark of the Covenant and the Wall of the Holy Temple which, like the Shechinah herself, are manifestations of God's presence in the world:

The wall is Master of all the earth, as it is written, "Behold, the Ark of the Covenant (of) the Master of all the earth." (Joshua 3:11) The Ark of the Covenant is the Shechinah, and is also called a wall, as in "a breaking down of walls." (Isaiah 22:5) Therefore, "Hezikiah turned his face toward the wall." He said in his prayer, "Remember now, Lord, I beseech you, how I have walked before you." (Isaiah 38:3) He declares that he has kept the holy covenant, and did not defile it but guarded it well, as it is written, "I have walked before you" and elsewhere "Walk before Me, and be perfect. And I will make my covenant. . . ." (Genesis 17:1–2)

Since all the females in the world are in the secret of the Shechinah, the Shechinah rests upon whomever has a wife, but not upon him who does not. Therefore, Hezikiah resolved to be purified before the Shechinah, and took it upon himself to marry. Then he "prayed to Hashem."

At the time he uttered this prayer, the Bible describes Hezikiah as being sick unto death. But he besought the Shechinah to bring a female presence into his life, and his prayer was answered. Hezikiah arose from his bed, found a wife, and God granted him fifteen more years on earth.

I am aware that to a contemporary reader this discussion of the Shechinah may seem skewed toward the male perspective. This can be explained without any need to patronize the Zohar as an artifact of a less progressive time and place. If the Shechinah seems less interested in women than men, it is because women simply do not need an infusion of female energy. They embody the potential for that energy to begin with, and they awaken it through acts of sharing and revealing light. Men, according to Kabbalah, require a female presence in order to manifest on any level in the physical world. If the emphasis on male viewpoints in these passages is an expression of gender bias, it could be argued that the bias is in favor of the female. Women carry within themselves what men must achieve outside.

CHAPTER 10

AFTER THE DELUGE: TEMPERANCE

The tragic "almost" is a poignant commonplace of epic literature. The *Iliad* tells how the Trojan War was almost brought to a close by a single combat between Paris and Menelaos. How many lives would have been spared had not Apollo intervened, and for the most petty of reasons! *Paradise Lost* shows us Satan seriously considering whether he is making a huge mistake by initiating the temptation in the garden ... but, alas, he decides to go ahead with it after all. But nowhere is this motif more forcefully present than in the biblical narrative. Since the Fall of Adam humanity has come close to ultimate fulfillment and redemption on several occasions. Even now just one small righteous action may be all that separates us from reentering Eden.

Noah certainly had his chance to restore Paradise on behalf of humanity. The Flood was like a huge *mikveh*—a ritual bath for all of creation, in which evil was subjected to a series of irresistible hot and cold "washing cycles."

Vol. 2, pp. 388–390

Rabbi Yehuda said that in Gehenom the wicked are punished with water for six months and with fire for six months. Why during the flood were they punished only by water for twelve months? Six months should have been enough. Rabbi Yosi told him that they were sentenced to both punishments: water and fire. The water that fell upon them from above was cold as snow. And they were also punished by fire, because the water that spouted from the deep was scalding. Thus, they were punished for twelve months, receiving the full sentence of Gehenom. This continued until they were completely removed from the face of the world. During this time, Noah was hidden in the ark. As a result, the Angel of Darkness did not approach him, and the ark roamed upon the waters, as it is written: "And they bore up the ark, and it was lifted above the earth." (Genesis 7:17)

The ark was lifted so high because, as we recall, in those days, "giants were on the earth." The people of the wicked generation were so large that one hundred fifty feet of water had to fall, covering even the tallest of the giants by at least thirty feet.

But when at last the waters had receded, Noah made a tragic mistake. It was, in fact, the same mistake Adam had made, and it came about in much the same way. Popular belief to the contrary, the forbidden fruit that tempted Adam and Eve was not an apple. It was a grape.

Come and behold: Adam's wife pressed him grapes and brought death upon him, Israel, and the whole world. When Noah came upon these grapes, he was not well guarded, as it is written: "He drank of the wine, and was drunk; and he was uncovered within his tent." (Genesis 9:21)

Some even say that Noah had found the very vine that had borne that fateful grape.

> "And Noah, a man of the earth, began and planted a vineyard." (Genesis 9:20) Rabbi Yehuda and Rabbi Yosi disagreed over interpretation of this verse. One said the vine had been thrown out of the Garden of Eden, and that Noah planted it in the ground. The other said that the vine had already been in the ground and Noah plucked it out and replanted it. It blossomed and gave fruit on the same day. He squeezed the grapes, drank their wine, and became drunk.

As he demonstrated in his verbal exchange with Eve in the Garden, the Angel of Darkness tailors his pitch to his audience. Perhaps out of consideration for Noah's year on a boat full of animals, the Angel used a lamb, a lion, a monkey, and a pig to seal his bond with Noah. It is said that just as Noah was planting the vine he had found, the Angel of Darkness appeared carrying a lamb under his arm. He slaughtered the lamb and allowed its blood to flow over the newly planted vine. Then he departed, but returned after a time with a lion, with which he performed the very same ritual. And he repeated it twice more, with a monkey and a pig.

All this was puzzling to Noah, but in truth the Angel was presenting him with an allegory of exactly what was about to happen. He was showing how self-serving desire carried to excess becomes self-destruction. With respect to wine, one cup makes us docile as a lamb. Then, after two cups, we may believe ourselves to be as powerful as the king of beasts. But it is all downhill from there. Soon enough we are making monkeys of ourselves, until before we know it we are rolling around in the mud like pigs. It is the potable

version of the "second bite" syndrome that befell Adam—and as in
the earlier instance, nakedness emerges as a theme. But while
Adam and Eve realized they were naked and covered themselves,
Noah went in the opposite direction. He took off his clothes and
lay on the floor of his tent.

> Rabbi Shimon said that Noah had come to reexamine
> Adam's sin so that he could refrain from repeating it
> and could make reparations in the world. But he was
> unable to accomplish this, because after squeezing the
> grapes in order to examine them, he became drunk,
> was uncovered, and had no strength to get up. This is
> why the verse reads, "and he was uncovered," meaning
> that he "uncovered" a Gap in the World which had
> been covered until that time.

Noah had started out with the best intentions. He thought he
was performing an experiment of sorts, "reexamining Adam's sin" at
this very important moment when the world had been cleansed and
purified to a point where it was literally good as new. But as many
dabblers in exotic substances were to learn in generations yet un-
born, Noah soon found himself engaged in more than detached observation.

Grapes, or the wine that comes from them, are a powerful and
potentially dangerous presence in the kabbalistic worldview. Wine
is central to the celebration of *Shabbat* and other holidays, but it is
also the object of many carefully delineated restrictions and prohi-
bitions. Wine puts us in touch with levels of consciousness outside
our everyday experience. We must prepare the vessels of our being
to receive the wine, just as we must prepare ourselves to receive the
Light. Wine can be thought of as a kind of superconductor that in-

tensifies the Light passing into us through the spiritual circuitry. Noah's error, like Adam's, was in creating a connection to the Light that he was inadequately prepared to sustain.

Kabbalah teaches that wine derives from the *Sefirah* of *Tiferet,* representing balance. We can benefit from wine when we use it with balance. Just as wine can bring overpowering energy into us, Kabbalah teaches that it can also deplete us when it is used unwisely. Thus, the numerological value of the Hebrew word for wine, *yayin,* equals seventy, the same value as *sod,* the word for secret. An old saying further hints at an unbalanced relationship between these two words: "When wine comes in, secrets go out."

Traditionally, drinking in the company of unrighteous or unobservant people has been especially proscribed. Pouring wine among the wrong company can lead to the pouring out of one's soul—not just verbally, but also in the sense of squandering the essence of our being. Since Noah's drinking partner after the Flood was none other than the Angel of Destruction, it is hardly surprising that we are still dealing with "the morning after."

What next took place in Noah's tent is one of the most puzzling and even shocking moments in the Zohar, or in all of spiritual literature.

> "And he drank of the wine, and was drunk, and he was uncovered." (Genesis 9:21) This aroused Cham, the father of Canaan, and he castrated Noah, thereby removing the secret of the Covenant, which had made Noah a righteous man. He removed the male organ, the means of begetting, which is given only by the power of the holy covenant. This is why Noah said, "Cursed be Canaan," because curses were initially brought upon the world by Canaan. For he is the secret of the serpent, as it is written: "A slave of slaves he shall be," and,

also, "Cursed are you of all cattle." (Genesis 3:14)
Everything shall be corrected in the future except for
Canaan. All the slaves except Canaan shall be freed
from their slavery. This is the secret known to those
who are familiar with the ways and the paths of the
Torah.

Again we notice a reprise of the Adam and Eve story, in which
family blood was shed by Cain, the son who slew his brother. Here
a son assaults his father, and in an especially violent way, especially
when we recall that Noah had been born circumcised, with the
mark of the Covenant already inscribed in his flesh. The comparison with Cain could hardly be more explicit in this text: If we fail
to understand Ham's (Cham) act as nearly identical to Cain's, then
Noah's curse of Canaan must alert us to the connection.

Vol. 2, p. 321

Rabbi Chiya and Rabbi Yosi were on their way, when
they came upon the mountains of Ararat and observed
some deep ravines that had been left from the days of
the Flood. Rabbi Chiya said: "The Creator has left
these ravines to stay on through all the generations,
so that the sins of the wicked would not be erased. Because as the Creator desires that the righteous should
be remembered, likewise he desires that the wicked
who do not fulfill his will should be remembered. He
desires that their sins never be forgotten, and their
punishments and their wicked ways always be remembered, as it is written, 'The stain of your iniquity remains before me.'" (Jeremiah 2:22)

In any case, it was another missed opportunity. The Vessel of humanity was not yet ready. And the Creator wants us to learn a lesson from this. In the study of Kabbalah and the Zohar, we begin to see that any activity that connects us with another dimension of consciousness—be it drink, drugs, sex, meditation, or prayer—draws Light to us. Rarely, if ever, is abstention recommended by the Zohar in regard to any of these vehicles. Rather we are guided to recognize temperance as the appropriate approach. To deserve a greater amount of Light we must work on and strengthen our spiritual Vessel. If we allow ourselves to "imbibe" large amounts of Light without having done that work, we will not be able to contain what we receive. We will become "drunk," incapacitated, and allow chaos free rein. Noah's sin was not in the physical act of drinking, but in drinking's metaphorical connotations. His drunkenness represented connection to a more intense level of Light than his spiritual Vessel could tolerate. In the biblical narrative and in human history as a whole, Noah was by no means the last person to make that mistake.

CHAPTER 11

THE RED SEA: CERTAINTY

There is only one premise in the whole of Kabbalah: The Creator is all-inclusive and lacks nothing whatsoever. The Creator is therefore good, since all aspects of evil stem from a feeling of lack. We can see this in our own lives, where all our jealousy, anger, and hatred result from frustrated desires for emotional or physical gratification. Having said that the Creator is complete and therefore good, we can now go on to describe the attribute of sharing through which we are aware of the Creator's existence.

We know from our own lives that giving and sharing is an attribute of goodness. If we consider any object or person we would call good, we realize that the essential quality all good things have in common is that they give us something we want. It might be something tangible, as in material gifts or an experience that gives us pleasure, or it might be something emotional, intellectual, or spiritual. It might also be survival itself, as in the biblical episode at the Red Sea.

When the Creator led the people out of Egypt he did not take them on the shortest route. The most direct way to travel from Egypt to what is now Israel is northeast, through the land of the Philistines. But the Creator led the Israelites due east instead.

Exodus 13:17

And it came to pass, when Pharaoh had let the people go, that God led them not through the way of the Land of the Philistines, although that was near; for He said, "Lest the people repent when they see war, and they return to Egypt." But He led the people about, through the way of the wilderness of the Red Sea. . . .

Why would God, after all their years in exile, make the former slaves travel a longer route to the Promised Land? The simple answer is that they had to go to the Red Sea in order for the defining miracle in Kabbalah to take place. The parting of the Red Sea is discussed at many points in the Zohar, but there is no section that seems to be the definitive exposition of the incident. It is so important that awareness of it is assumed to be everywhere. But its true significance is not what the average reader might expect.

The Zohar dramatically sets the scene as the people reach the water's edge.

Vol. 9, pp. 210–212

At that moment, the children of Israel saw trouble on all sides. The sea with its towering waves was in front of them, all these multitudes and all the camps of Egypt were behind them, and above there were many Prosecutors against them. They started to cry to the Holy One, blessed be He.

Then it is written: "And Hashem said to Moshe, 'Why do you cry to Me?'" (Exodus 14:15) We learned at that moment the Light was revealed, goodwill was present in all the worlds above, and then the collective Light shone.

"Why do you cry to me?" would seem to be a strange response from a God who intends what is best for His chosen people. Yet contained within that response is the essence of kabbalistic teaching. The Creator is saying, "It's up to you. Your salvation depends on your taking action in the physical world." But there is nothing light about this pronouncement. If we start from the certainty that God wants no harm to come to us, we can discover in His response the idea that *we have everything we need* to save ourselves, if only we choose to make use of these tools. More specifically, Kabbalah teaches that God has provided us with the implements of our own salvation. They are nothing other than the tools of Kabbalah itself, including prayer, meditation, the Sabbath, and most especially the Zohar.

From a practical standpoint, we must have certainty not in the Creator and His ability to protect and care for us, but in the efficacy of the tools that He has provided for us. Certainty in the Creator Himself is first and foremost an internal condition—a state of mind. The tools require action. The midrash teaches that when Moses stretched out his hand over the waters, nothing happened. It was only when one man actually walked out into the waves that the Red Sea parted—but not until the water had reached his neck and he kept walking. Then and only then was certainty in the tools of Kabbalah really made manifest.

Through the study of Kabbalah, these principles are accessible to all. We can connect with the world of certainty and order and leave behind the illusory world of chaos and disorder. With perfect clarity, Kabbalah and the Zohar can lead us to a level of fulfillment that we have never before encountered.

However it may sometimes seem in our daily lives, we have an orderly universe around us. Before we can live in this universe in a meaningful way, however, we should rid ourselves of the belief that we are helpless human beings about to drown in a stormy sea. We must assure ourselves that we will master the course of our lives. The Zohar restores this consciousness to the central position in our lives. Through reading and scanning the Zohar, we tunnel through space and time, traveling at the speed of light toward transformation. The Tree-of-Life reality unfolds before our eyes.

Coming to grips with these seemingly outlandish notions strains the imagination. And yet Kabbalah teaches that, for those who use its tools, the truth always turns out to be more wonderful than anything we could have imagined.

The following passage makes an astonishing point.

> Rabbi Yitzchak said: "Then, when everything shone together, the sea executed the supernal laws—the commandment to save Israel—because those above and those below were given over to it. Therefore, we say that raising children, longevity, and sustenance are as difficult before the Creator as the splitting of the Red Sea."

Here this account of a great miracle subverts the very idea of miracles. A monumental occurrence is compared to the doings of everyday life. This, however, is not a downgrading of what took place during the Exodus; it is an elevation of the basic challenges of being alive. Miracles are not about extraordinary happenings. They are about the connection to the Light that makes the extraordinary possible, and the (seemingly) ordinary as well. In this sense, the Zohar tells us, raising children is a miracle. So is just staying alive.

> Rabbi Shimon said: "There is one deer on earth and the Creator does much for her. When she cries, the Creator hearkens to her distress and listens to her

voice. And when the world needs Mercy in relation to water, she utters voice and the Creator hearkens to her voice. Then He has pity on the world, as is written: 'As the hart pants after the water brooks.' " (Psalms 42:2)

When she needs to give birth, she is stopped from all sides. She places her head between her knees, cries, and screams, and the Creator has pity on her. He sends a snake that bites her genitals and opens her and tears that place for her, and she gives birth immediately. Rabbi Shimon said: "In this matter do not question and do not test God. For this is exactly so."

With its characteristic juxtaposition of gentle and aggressive images, the Zohar reveals God's mercy through violence. This, after all, is what took place at the Red Sea as well. In fact, it is taking place all around us at every moment, though most of us choose to turn away. Let us, instead, step out into the waves. The Zohar cautions us not to test God. Let us therefore test ourselves.

Part Three

TRANSFORMATIONS

CHAPTER 12

ADAM'S REPENTANCE

Kabbalah teaches that two parallel universes are available to us. The first is the realm of the Tree of Knowledge, introduced in the book of Genesis, into which we entered as a result of Adam's sin. A second realm is that of the Tree of Life, which only Kabbalah and the Zohar clearly define. The domain of the Tree of Life is a realm free of all pain and suffering. When we connect with this reality, we leave the familiar chaotic landscape in which the seemingly insurmountable problems of life surround us. And it can be done!

Until recently, the idea of parallel universes would have been difficult for most people to understand, much less to accept as scientifically validated. Yet at the time of this writing, one of the most influential theories describing the universe is the so-called many worlds interpretation. This proposes not just two, but an infinite number of universes endlessly coming into being to provide for all the possible alternatives of every event, from the largest to the seemingly least significant. In comparison, the teachings of Kabbalah are amazingly clear. We can all relate to circumstances that foster a joyous consciousness within us. Most of us also have first-hand knowledge of another aspect of our nature, one that we prefer to experience as infrequently as possible. These two dimensions exist side by side. They are nothing less than opposite realities.

Kabbalah's understanding of the Adam and Eve story is founded on this notion of parallel universes. Some biblical commentaries present Adam and Eve as genuine historical figures, while others see them as the symbolic protagonists of a folktale or creation myth. For the sages of Kabbalah, the story is both a historical account and a rich source of information about the secrets of Creation. Most important, the account of Adam and Eve is a compendium of mystical codes that the Zohar deciphers. In particular, from the dialog between Eve and the serpent the Zohar derives concealed information about the parallel realities that lie before us.

Genesis 3:1–4

And the Lord commanded Adam, of every tree from the garden you may eat. However, from the Tree of Knowledge of Good and Evil, do not eat thereof, for on the day that you eat from it, you shall surely die. And the snake said to the woman, did the Lord say, you shall not eat of any tree from the garden? And the woman said to the snake, from the fruit of any tree we can eat. From the fruit of the tree in the center of the garden [Tree of Knowledge] God said we shall not eat of it nor touch it, for we shall assuredly die, and the snake said to the woman, you assuredly will not die.

With all the respect due to scripture, this story immediately raises a very straightforward question: *Does it make any sense?* The Creator told Adam that if he ate from the Tree of Knowledge he "would surely die." The serpent said that God was wrong, and, in fact, after Adam and Eve sinned and ate from the Tree of Knowledge, they did not immediately die. Adam lived to the age of 930 years. I am puzzled that throughout my early years of biblical study, the apparent error of the Creator's pronouncement was never explored or even mentioned. Nor did I myself bring it up. Presumably it existed in the domain of things that were never to be questioned.

But no such domain exists in Kabbalah or in the Zohar. It is a fundamental rule of kabbalistic study that *everything* in the Torah must be questioned, and there are several reasons for this. On a societal level, the author of the Zohar recognized that absolute scriptural authority can be abusive and can extend beyond the boundaries of study and worship. This can come about only when inquiry is stifled and ignorance flourishes. But there is an even more important spiritual imperative to question the Torah. As the Zohar puts it, "Those who consider the stories of the Torah to indicate merely a story alone are foolish and uninformed. For if that were the case, then the supernal Torah, which is full of holiness and truth, could have been written by anyone who was qualified to write beautiful stories."

So let us consider a kabbalistic interpretation of the story. In the Garden of Eden, Adam and Eve lived in the domain of the Tree of Life. Their state of being was sustained and nourished by an aspect of the Creator's Light that provided a wholly beneficent environment, absolutely harmonious and free from chaos of any sort. Moreover, before they connected to the Tree-of-Knowledge reality, they maintained a consciousness of certainty about their state of existence. This certainty was essential to their presence in the universe of the Tree of Life. Were that certainty to falter, they would enter a new reality dominated by doubt.

When Adam and Eve partook of the Tree of Knowledge, they severed their connection with the domain of "mind over matter." The Tree of Knowledge represented a universe dominated by uncertainty. It was the domain of the adversary, of the negative side. Here certainty was eroded, and even "belief" was hard to come by. Connecting with the Tree of Knowledge brought chaos, pain, and death.

When the Creator told Adam and Eve not to eat from the Tree of Knowledge, this was an injunction for them to maintain their consciousness in the realm of the Tree of Life. Immortality was their birthright, but connecting with the Tree of Knowledge would bring first uncertainty, and then the mortality upon which it is grounded. In the Garden of Eden incident, both the serpent and the Lord were correct. But the serpent's perspective was short term rather than eternal. It was true that Adam and Eve did not immediately die, but the Creator had been speaking in a different context. Connecting with the Tree of Knowledge would bring about a death consciousness that would eventually manifest on the physical plane. But one thing was now certain, and only one thing. It was the loss of certainty itself.

While the Bible compresses and abbreviates relentlessly, the Zohar interprets, expands, and expatiates. The Zohar not only decodes the narrative and themes of the Bible but also reveals the true character of the biblical personages, including the Creator Himself. In the Zohar, the Creator is revealed as the loving and thoroughly benevolent Father of all humanity.

Vol. 2, pp. 248–252

When Adam sinned the Creator was saddened, because Adam had now justified the question the angels had put to Him: "What is this man that you are mindful of him, and the son of man that you visit him?" (Psalms 8:4)

Rabbi Yehuda said, "The Creator was grieved to His heart because He had to execute judgment upon His creation, because He was destroying the work of His hands for Israel.

"It was the same way when Israel crossed the Red Sea. The angels came to sing before the Creator, and

He said to them: 'Behold, you are singing and the work
of my hands is drowning!' For even when the wicked
are taken out of this world, He is saddened."

Throughout the Bible and the commentaries, facets of the
Creator's nature are signified by the different names ascribed to
Him. In particular, *Adonai* refers to His merciful aspect, while *Elohim* denotes the energy of judgment or necessary severity. The
Zohar depicts the Creator as always troubled by the need to mete
out judgment. His inclination is toward kindness, and when He
does inflict punishment He almost always looks for a way to soften
it, even when the edict is well deserved. Everything in Creation,
after all, is the work of His hand, and every detail of the universe
was composed in perfect harmony. Thus, the Bible refers to the
divine order of creation as a song (*shirah*). The slightest alteration
upsets the exquisite melody, as it is written, "Do not add to the
word that I am commanding you, and do not subtract from it."
(Deuteronomy 4:2) Even the purveyors of evil have their place, and
when harm comes to them they are mourned by God.

Rabbi Aba said that the Creator was grieved when
Adam sinned before Him and transgressed His commands. The Creator said to Adam: "Woe to you who
have weakened the heavenly power." For at that moment a light was extinguished, and forthwith Adam
was banished from the Garden of Eden.

At the instant of Adam's sin, the divine presence in the universe
was diminished. It is said that when Adam viewed the first sunset,
he was frightened, believing that this symbol of what the Zohar
calls "heavenly power" was disappearing forever, and that the world

would be permanently trapped in darkness. As with the sunset, however, the extinguishing of the divine Light is temporary, and is necessary for us to appreciate what Light really means. The dawn cannot come to pass without twilight, and the transformation of humanity cannot take place without the Fall.

This is only an analogy, however, and not a perfect one. We know how long a night will last, but how much time will the transformation of humanity require? How many eons will pass before the Tree-of-Life reality is reestablished? The answer is really up to us. The kabbalists teach that transformation could happen tomorrow, or today. By making use of the divinely given tools of Kabbalah, we reveal Light in the world and hasten the return to Eden—and a whole genre of kabbalistic stories describe how close humanity has already come to achieving this. Again and again, the stories tell us, the redemption of the world could have been achieved. If just one person had made a positive choice in a seemingly insignificant circumstance, the ruby gates of the Garden of Eden would have swung open.

> The Creator said to him: "I placed you in the Garden to make offerings, and you have impaired the altar so that offerings cannot be brought upon it. Therefore go forth and work the land."

So many concepts are expressed in these few lines. Kabbalistically, the idea that Adam was "placed in the garden" means that he was created at the highest level of being. Oneness with God was his; there was no spiritual distance between the Creator and His Creation. But Adam's fall damaged this connection. His sin shorted out the metaphysical circuitry so that the Vessel could no longer receive the full force of the Creator's Light, and it moved Adam back to the *Sefirah* of *Malchut*, the material level of being. Once the meaning of this is understood, the Creator's admonition to Adam becomes clear. "Go and work the land" is not a curse or a criminal sentence. It is a logical directive for the level of being on which Adam now exists. *Since you are no longer on the highest level of spiritual connection,* the Creator is saying, *you must now do your spiritual work through the physical dimension—that is, "the land." You must rebuild the Vessel of yourself through your own work in the world.*

> And the Creator decreed that Adam should die. Taking pity on him, however, the Creator allowed him to be buried close to the entrance of the Garden of Eden, where Adam had made a cave in which he hid himself with his wife. How did Adam know to choose this place? Because a faint ray of Light from the Garden entered there, and therefore he desired to be buried in the cave.
>
> Come and behold: no one leaves this world without seeing Adam. He asks each person for what reason he departs this life, and in what state his soul takes leave of it. And each person replies: "Woe to you, that because of you I have to die." To which Adam replies: "My son, I have transgressed but one commandment, and I have been punished for doing so. As for you, consider how many transgressions of the Creator's precepts you have committed!"

Although it was Adam's sin that brought death into the world, Adam is not responsible for our individual deaths. When (or if) we die, we ourselves bear the responsibility, and in fact there are a few great souls who have avoided death altogether. This passage discusses the Creator's steps to allay Adam's fears. The sages tell us that after a dying person hears Adam speak the lines quoted in the preceding passage, he or she is caused to create a written record of any and all transgressions committed during their lifetime. This document is then closed with a seal that will remain unbroken until the final judgment, whereupon it will be opened and we will all be judged according to our own words. Underlying this teaching is the precept that we must accept responsibility for *everything* that comes into our lives, even our own death. How easy this is to say, but how difficult to achieve! It is the mark of a *tzaddik* to recognize adversity as an opportunity to show love and trust in God. It is the sign of a righteous person to reject the temptations of victimhood, even for a moment—and especially at the last moment, for the nature of our consciousness at that instant expresses the total spiritual achievement of our lives.

> Rabbi Chiya said: "To this very day, Adam twice each day confesses his sins to the patriarchs. He shows them the very place in the Garden where he resided in supernal glory before his fall. Each day he also gazes upon his righteous descendants who have attained the glory of the Garden of Eden that once was his, and they praise the Creator, saying: 'How precious is your kindness! The children of man take refuge under the shadow of your wings.' " (Psalms 36:8)

The Zohar provides a detailed description of the order of merit of the souls who have entered Paradise, from the great biblical figures to the martyrs to the "righteous poor" who made an effort to study sacred books. A high place in this hierarchy is accorded to penitents. This might be expected in light of the preceding passage, and we have seen elsewhere that sincere repentance pleases the Creator more than unfailing righteousness.

Given the Zohar's emphasis on this teaching, it is also important to note that when the great sage and martyr Rabbi Akiva ben Joseph was asked if there was any sinner who could not be forgiven, he specified "those who repent too much" and "those who sin with the intention of repenting." We cannot manipulate the kindness of God. We must not misconstrue Kabbalah's teachings on repentance as a license to do anything and everything, since the Creator will forgive us whenever we want.

The world is not a theme park, in which the challenges are make-believe and we are guaranteed a manageable outcome for the price of a ticket. The truth is both "better" and "worse" than that. We are guaranteed not only a manageable outcome, but a reentry to Paradise. And we print our own ticket through our spiritual work.

CHAPTER 13

NOAH

What is it in our spiritual nature that prevents us from exercising the great power that lies within us? There seems to be a fundamental difference between the way an instinct toward spiritual transformation is activated in the human soul, and the arousal of other forms of strength and capability. When someone has the potential to be a great athlete, even the first indications of developing skill are enough to stimulate diligent practice. A child who runs fast soon notices that a little consistent effort allows him or her to run even faster, and the pleasure inherent in this creates motivation toward further progress. In a similar way, highly intelligent people seem to enjoy using their intelligence, especially if they believe they have real intellectual ability. Research in social psychology has clearly demonstrated this principle. When students are told by their instructor that an examination will be easy for them and that they definitely have the intellectual tools to succeed, those students consistently perform better than others who are presented with a more pessimistic outlook. In fact, confidence of success produced by simple encouragement is one of the most powerful elements in all forms of achievement— except, it seems, in our spiritual work.

Kabbalah assures us that, if we will just use the tools the Creator has provided, we cannot fail in the task of self-transformation. Yet many people hesitate. They feel that they are beyond redemption, that there is no option left in their lives beyond wondering, "What's the use?" Kabbalah views this as a fundamental error, and one of the most powerful tactics of the negative side.

We ourselves, and no one else, are responsible for the distance and the obstacles that exist between us and the Creator. We have fabricated those obstacles out of the very desire that was intended to connect us with God. Out of the sharing energy with which the Creator intended that we should be closer to Him than the angels, we have allowed a negative power to take hold. We feel drawn and attached to foolish things. Out of the very power that could enable us to feel the love of God as the angels do, we fashion fear, anger, and illusion.

In this book we have often referred to the teachings of Kabbalah, but we must remember that we are nonetheless the best educators of ourselves. We must take the teachings and the tools into our own hands and realize that we are the captains of our own ships, or we may founder and even drown in the sea of the material world and its deluded aspirations.

This point is made very well through a humorous anecdote I have often told to new Kabbalah students. In a remote part of the country a huge rain began to fall. It seemed to be the biggest deluge since Noah, and flooding began very quickly. When the water was about six inches deep throughout the county, the state police gave orders that the entire area had to be evacuated. But when the police arrived at an isolated farmhouse to give the order, they found the farmer sitting calmly on his front porch with no intention of leaving. "The Lord will save me," he said.

Some time later, when the water was several feet deep, the police returned in a rowboat to evacuate the farmer. This time they found him sitting on the roof of his house, and he still intended to stay right where he was. "The Lord will save me," he repeated.

But the rain still continued. With the water now over higher than the roofs of most houses, the police used a helicopter in a last attempt to rescue the farmer. They found him standing on the top of his chimney, the only part of his home that was still above the flood. He glanced at the helicopter and shook his head. "The Lord will save me," he declared. But a short time later he drowned.

Now, as he found himself before the throne of heaven, the farmer was puzzled and somewhat indignant about what had happened. He addressed the Creator with definite impatience in his voice. "I was so sure you would save me," he lamented. "What happened?"

And the Creator's voice thundered, "Who do you think sent the police car, the rowboat, and the helicopter?"

Using humor, this story makes some extremely important points. The heavy rain is not intrinsically evil. If there were no houses, farms, or other man-made enterprises, the rain would be an entirely neutral phenomenon. In fact, it would probably have many long-term benefits for the soil and the water table. But the effects of a huge rain are not neutral in the world we live in, so we must assume responsibility and take action. We must understand that "acts of God" that seem to originate "out of the blue" come from the Creator. Even inner qualities that we ourselves may recognize as evil are, in their essence and their origin, shining Lights of the Divine that have been drawn down through the *Sefirot* and have become part of our being. We must grasp this fact in order to undertake the process of spiritual repair that Kabbalah calls *tikkun*. As in any kind of healing, the first step is recognizing the source of the disease, which very often is the receptive environment for illness that we have created in ourselves. If we fail to understand this or fail to act accordingly, this omission is an act of free will, and our own responsibility.

With the story of Noah, the Zohar confronts the difficult life of a righteous man in a corrupt environment, and the obstacles he encountered in striving to serve God. These obstacles existed in his own heart as well as in the outer world. To be sure, it all began well enough. Noah's birth brought an end to the curse the Creator had put on the land at the time of Adam's expulsion from the Garden. Ten generations had passed since then, and according to scripture "ten is consecrated to God." (Leviticus 27:33) Therefore, Noah was born with the divine covenant already expressed in his body as well as in his soul.

Vol. 2, pp. 259–260

Come and see what was said of Noah: "And he called his name Noah saying, he shall comfort us from our work." (Genesis 5:29) How was it understood that Noah would bring comfort as soon as he was born? When the Creator cursed the world, saying, "The land will be cursed because of you," Adam asked, "How long will the world be subject to this curse?" The Creator replied, "Until you beget a son who is born circumcised like yourself."

When Noah was born, Adam saw that he was circumcised and transcribed with a sacred sign. And when he saw that the Shechinah embraced the baby, he named him in anticipation of what would come to pass.

At first, no one knew how to sow, reap, or plow.

They worked the earth with their hands. Then Noah came and crafted the tools needed for working the ground so that it would bear fruit. Before he came, people sowed wheat and reaped thorns and thistles. Noah liberated the earth from its curse. Hence, he was called "a man of the ground." (Genesis 8:21)

Until Noah's birth, with the force of God's judgment still in effect, there could be no agriculture. Kabbalistically, this means that spiritual progress could not take place in the "ground state" of the physical world. Noah's designation as "a man of the ground" refers in part to the healing effect of his presence on an entire level of being. In a sense, he was a second Adam. He came to initiate and preside over an environment of rejuvenated abundance. Indeed, Noah had the power to consummate the spiritual transformation of humanity. But he proved to be only one important step in that journey. The sages liken this process to the creation of a garden. Adam was the force that caused rain to fall and allowed plants to germinate. Noah brought the tools needed to tend the garden. It would not be until the appearance of Abraham that the true blossoming could take place.

In kabbalistic terms, Noah personifies the *Sefirah* of *Yesod*. He is the connection between *Malchut*, the physical dimension, and the Upper Worlds of the other *Sefirot*. But as in the narrative of the primordial Light and Vessel, the physical realm in Noah's time was still unprepared to receive a sudden and full infusion of the Creator's Light. From drought and deprivation, Kabbalah teaches that humanity abruptly entered a period of exaggerated fertility, in which crops sprang from the earth at the instant the seeds were planted. Among the angels, there were some who loved this abundance. They forsook heaven, descended to the physical world, and intermingled with human beings. This gave rise to a race of giants

(Genesis 6:4), whose prodigious strength created an environment of arrogant license.

Vol. 2, pp. 276–279

> One day Rabbi Chiya and Rabbi Yosi were walking. Reaching some great mountains, they found human bones that belonged to the generation of the Flood. They walked alongside one of these bones, which measured three hundred paces. Astonished, they said to each other: "This clarifies what our friends have said, how that generation did not fear the divine judgment!"

Among these corrupt beings, "Noah found grace in the eyes of the Creator." (Genesis 6:8) He occupies a special place among the biblical personalities, and, if such a thing is possible, he could even be described as a controversial patriarch. Much of the controversy centers on Genesis 6:9: "Noah was a righteous man, and perfect in his generations." According to one interpretation, this means that Noah's perfection was only in comparison to the depravity of the people of his era—with the corollary idea that Noah would have been less exceptional if he had lived in the time of Abraham or Moses. On the other hand, perhaps Noah was like a great athlete whose career was stunted by the limitations of his teammates. It is believed he would have been even greater if he had lived in a more spiritually elevated generation.

The spiritual merit of succeeding generations is a frequently explored topic in the literature of Kabbalah. Earlier generations, like children, were closer to God in the sense that Creation had more recently taken place. Being closer to the source of spirituality, they needed less from the physical world. This pertained not only to luxuries and the trappings of wealth, but even to sacred books and teachings. Yet they were more gifted in the working of wonders and miracles than even the most enlightened figures of more recent times. They were on a higher plane of existence, able to maintain their elevated status and exert control over the direction of the world through their spirituality. This control expressed itself in dramatic manifestations of their power over the physical world. If it appears that high attainments and diligent study are less rewarded than merely being alive in the biblical period, Kabbalah explains this as a function of the spiritual levels inherent in different generations.

Nowadays we must rely to a greater extent on knowledge from secondary sources, such as the written word. Yet our lack of intrinsic spiritual powers, and the greater intensity of desire that may grow out of this, makes us more capable of receiving the Light. The Vessels of ourselves may be of a coarser material, but their power to reveal the Light has never been greater, not even in the time of Abraham.

> Rabbi Elazar asked, "What is the meaning of 'his generations'?" This refers to the descendants who issued from him, all of whom he perfected through his righteousness, and by whom he in turn was also perfected.
>
> The Creator praised him twice, calling him, "Noah, Noah." (Genesis 6:9) But if he had lived in another generation, such as that of Abraham or King David or Moses, perhaps he would not have been considered at all. Yet another explanation is this: with all that he was able to perform in a generation in which all were wicked, how much more he could have done in a generation in which all were righteous.

When the Creator saw the sinfulness that afflicted the world, He chose to impose judgment. But this is never done precipitously or without reluctance, and He always makes His intentions well known:

> The Creator said: "I will destroy man whom I have created from the face of the earth." (Genesis 6:7) Rabbi Yosi quotes: "For my thoughts are not your thoughts." (Isaiah 55:8) Come and see: when a man wants to take vengeance on another, he says nothing. If he discloses his intentions, his opponent will be on guard.
>
> But the Creator does not execute judgment on the world before he declares himself once, twice, three times. No one can reproach him, nor guard against him, nor resist him.
>
> The Creator said: "I will destroy man whom I have created from the face of the earth." Through Noah he announced these words. He warned the people several times but they did not listen, and he executed judgment against them.

God could have started the rain at any time. He certainly did not have to wait the 120 years required for Noah to build the ark, yet he did so as an expression of his mercy. Through all this time, the people of the world could have repented, and they did not.

Vol. 2, p. 299

> What is written about the generation of the Flood that did not repent? "And the Creator saw the earth, and behold, it was corrupt," like a wife who committed

adultery and hides her face from her husband. When the sins of mankind multiply and become overwhelming, the earth sins openly like a woman without shame. As it is written, "The earth was defiled under its inhabitants." (Isaiah 24:5)

It is also true, however, that Noah could have done more. He built the ark as God commanded, and he withstood the contempt of onlookers, but he did not attempt to intercede with the Creator on behalf of his fellow man. Abraham literally argued with God in an effort to save Sodom and Gomorrah. And Moses was prepared to give up his own life in exchange for the safety of the nation of Israel. Moreover, Moses was able to generate a supreme revelation of Light on Mount Sinai. The Tree-of-Life reality would have been restored but for the transgression of the golden calf. Noah was unable to accomplish such a feat in his time. On the other hand, Moses benefited from the spiritual force of the entire people of Israel, mobilized into a critical mass. Noah was a force of one. How much could be expected of him once the Divine power had turned to judgment?

Kabbalah teaches that under certain circumstances the power of the Angel of Darkness becomes vastly increased. When collective negative actions accumulate to a critical point, Death is granted free rein. Even innocent souls are subject to destruction. This was the case in Egypt during the tenth plague, when the firstborn of the oppressors died and the slaves were spared because of markings on their doorposts. During the Flood, only Noah and his family found refuge within the ark; no one else escaped.

According to kabbalistic teachings, the ark signifies *Malchut*, the physical world. Noah represents all the righteous souls who desire to construct the Vessel of themselves in order to receive the Light—and desire is the key word here. Noah, through his progeny, was able to beget children to repopulate the world. The work of the ark's construction represents the awakening of desire in *Malchut*, while Noah's offspring are manifestations of the Light revealed in the physical realm.

This is a symbolic interpretation; there is another one, more baroque and self-referential, in which the Zohar itself is an ark, providing protection and preservation in times of chaos and destruction. Within the Zohar's confines, a genuine desire for transforming our nature can ignite. The great teachers assure us that the Zohar is the most powerful of all kabbalistic tools for removing the negative inclinations born into the hearts of humanity.

CHAPTER 14

THE GENERATION OF THE FLOOD

Vol. 2, pp. 315–321

Noah warned the people of his generation, but they did not heed him until the Creator brought the punishment of Gehenom upon them. What is the punishment of Gehenom? It is ice and fire. The first is cold, the other boiling. And all of that generation were sentenced to punishment in Gehenom and were lost from the world.

The peculiar word *Gehenom* derives from the name of a valley outside Jerusalem that in ancient times was used as a garbage dump. Kabbalah, however, might describe it in more contemporary terms as a kind of spiritual recycling center, for every soul upon leaving this world must undergo the purification process of Gehenom. If a soul experiences this as pain and punishment, as many souls do, this is an expression of their own nature. On the other hand, there is the worthy minority who come through absolutely unscathed. They pass through very quickly on their way to the Garden of Eden, and the elevated nature of their being causes even the fires of the inferno to cool. The temperature of hell, it might be said, depends on where we ourselves set the thermostat. We may not realize it, but we are engaged in fine-tuning that setting at every moment of every day.

Through the work of Joseph Campbell, Mircea Eliade, and other scholars of comparative cultures, it has become clear that a particular culture's view of the afterlife—both as reward and as punishment—expresses that culture's values in terms of its experience in the physical world. To the peoples of the Arctic, for example, heaven is set in a temperate climate, while hell is unrelentingly cold. An opposite view prevails among the Bedouin tribes of the Sahara, with whom Western society shares the idea of a very hot hell. Kabbalah's depiction of hell is less visually oriented than that of other traditions. Gehenom, as the Zohar calls it, is described less graphically and more in terms of spiritual issues, in keeping with the principle that the physical dimension is always subordinate to metaphysical reality. This is made very clear in a fable I have told many times over the years. The fable concerns a man who was granted permission to visit both heaven and hell and returned to tell the tale.

> With an angel for his guide, the visitor is first ushered through the gates of Gehenom, which, he is surprised to find, are made of finely wrought gold. The gates, in fact, are incomparably lovely, as is the verdant landscape that lies beyond them. All this is quite astonishing to the visitor, who turns to his angelic guide in disbelief. "It's all so beautiful," the man says. "The sight of the meadows and mountains . . . the sounds of the birds singing in the trees . . . the scent of thousands of flowers. . . ." And then another scent catches his attention: the aroma of food being prepared.
>
> The angel leads the visitor toward an immense banquet table laden with every sort of delicacy. However, something is terribly wrong. Hundreds of people are

seated around the table, but they all appear to be starv-
ing. Their emaciated condition is painful to see in the
midst of such bounty, but even worse is the frustration
and anger they are obviously experiencing. Each person
at the table has a long-handled spoon chained to his
wrist. The handles are so long that no one can place
food in his mouth. But that does not prevent the condemned souls from trying. For all eternity, they are
struggling to feed themselves a meal that is right before
them, but that might as well be a hundred miles away.

Taken aback by the tragic spectacle, the visitor is
now more than ready to visit Paradise, and the angel
immediately complies. At once they pass through another set of golden gates, alike in every detail to the
gates of hell. In fact, a great deal about the two locales
seems to be identical, including the banquet table and
the diners chained to their utensils. But the people
around this table are well-fed and happy, despite the
fact that their circumstances are identical to those of
the damned. The difference is not in the physical situation, but in how they respond to it. As you might have
guessed by now, instead of trying to feed themselves,
each of the souls at this table feeds the one across the
table.

Versions of this story exist throughout world mythologies. It
could be understood as a version of the Greek myth of King Tan-
talus, the tyrant who in the afterlife was "tantalized" by food and
drink that were always just beyond his reach. But the kabbalistic
fable includes a crucial addition. We are given more than just the
sinners' punishment. The means of escape is presented also, and
it is almost frighteningly easy. On the whole, this story is a truly

elegant expression of the difference between desire to receive for the self alone and desire to receive for the purpose of sharing. I am aware of no other tale that better expresses this fundamental kabbalistic teaching—and we should not be surprised that this teaching occurs in a fable about Gehenom. For hell, according to Kabbalah, is a kind of didactic experience. It is educational in the etymological sense of the word, from the Latin *educare,* which itself is a contraction of *ex ducare,* meaning *to lead out of.* We are educated in hell. Like numerous other spiritual traditions, Kabbalah holds that individual souls may return to the material plane over and over until they achieve their corrections. So we souls are led out of darkness and cleansed for another incarnation, another chance to connect with the Light and achieve oneness with the Creator. The length of time that will be needed for cleansing, the number of lifetimes required in the world, and the difficulties encountered in either setting depends on no one but ourselves.

Have you now, like the man in the tale, had enough of Gehenom? Perhaps so, but let us linger another moment to invoke a contemporary representation of hell, and to note its congruence with Kabbalah's ancient teaching. Jean-Paul Sartre's autobiography is entitled *The Words,* and with good reason. Sartre wrote several million of them, of which perhaps the best known come from his play *No Exit:* "Hell is other people." As I interpret it, this refers not to the annoying habits of our fellow human beings, but to the sense of missed opportunity so powerfully conveyed in the preceding fable. Every person who comes into our lives represents a chance for growth, salvation, and fulfillment. But how often do we allow ourselves to take advantage of this opportunity? Instead, we give rein to our negative inclinations. The presence of other people in the world only drives us deeper into our ego-driven desires. As the fable depicts it, we keep trying to get for ourselves, when to give is the essence of freedom and fulfillment.

The experience of this—the frustration, anger, and envy—is hellish in itself. But hell really comes into being when we realize how easily it could all have been different. This painful recognition could be described as the reverse of wisdom, which Kabbalah defines as the power to discern the end in the beginning, to see the full-grown tree in the newly sown seed. Hell, on the other hand, is finally and belatedly recognizing the beginning in the end. Late in his life, T. S. Eliot observed (I am paraphrasing here) that the end of our journey is in arriving at the place we started and knowing it truly for the first time. To create a precise description of Gehenom, we need add only four words: "... *when it's too late.*" As the Zohar says, "Noah warned the people of his generation, but they did not heed him until the Creator brought the punishment of Gehenom upon them."

> Noah entered the ark and brought into it all the species
> of living creatures of the world. Noah was like a tree
> that begot fruit, when all the animals—big and small,
> in every variety—came forth from the ark. That is why
> Noah is called a "man of the ground."

Here again the Zohar's depiction of Noah at the time of the Flood recalls Adam in the Garden of Eden. We have referred to the Flood story as a kind of second Genesis, but there are important differences. More than was true of Adam, Noah is directly identified with the power of creation. Adam named the animals, but now the Zohar seems to depict them as somehow gestating a second time in the ark and then being reborn from it—and, by extension, being born from the man who created the ark. Adam existed in the presence of the Tree of Life, but Noah is represented as if he himself were the Tree, or even the ground from which the Tree arises.

To understand this, we must recall Kabbalah's teaching that the supremely righteous human beings known as *tzaddikim* are the true foundation of the world, the spiritual "ground" upon which everything is constructed. The world is here because of the *tzaddikim*. They perpetuate life at the spiritual level in the same way that oxygen sustains physical existence, and the story of Noah renders these ideas with a dreamlike concision of metaphor. Noah is spoken of as a tree, and the ark is of course made of wood. Noah constructs the ark, but he also is the ark. He sustains life by what he does as an artisan, and also by what he is as a *tzaddik*.

> For 300 years before the Flood, Noah warned the people to change their ways. . . . But they followed the evil inclination. They held fast to its trunk and roots, and became defiled. So it is written, "The end of all flesh has come before me." (Genesis 6:13)
>
> Rabbi Yehuda related this verse to one reading, "Lord, make me know my end and the measure of my days." (Psalms 9:5) There are "two ends," two paths for man to walk to the World of Truth—one on the right and one on the left.
>
> King David said to the Creator, "What is the portion of my lot?" (Psalms 39:5) And he had no rest until he was told, "Sit at my right hand." (Psalms 110:1) When the Creator told Noah, "The end of all flesh has come before me," Noah asked, "Which end? The end of the right or the end of the left?" The Creator answered, "It is the end that brought darkness upon the faces of the creatures." That is, it was the end of the left, which is the Angel of Darkness.

Ultimately, according to Kabbalah, every soul is destined for peace, joy, and the fulfillment that accompanies oneness with the

Creator. In this sense, "All roads lead to Rome." But while some of us will take the Appian Way, others will choose a mud-clogged path. In the process of spiritual transformation, some will use the tools of Kabbalah that the Creator has provided for us, and some will reach the same objective by following what the sages call "the path of torment."

The revelation of the Light within us, in other words, can be accomplished in two ways. One is trial and error, with the seeker tossing about on the seas of this world, grasping at new lifestyles, philosophies, diets, and doctrines as if they were pieces of driftwood floating past. Though not insurmountable, the odds against finding spiritual fulfillment in this manner are monumental.

A far less haphazard approach develops from an understanding of the process of mental, emotional, and spiritual evolution as revealed by Kabbalah and the Zohar. Ultimate reality is hidden from our view by a fog of negativity, conflict, and unsatisfied desire. Through Kabbalah we can penetrate that fog as if with a powerful searchlight. We can glimpse the primordial origins of ourselves, in the time when we lived in unity with the Light. By so doing, we can learn to connect with the Light anew.

This is an extremely important teaching. At literally every moment of our existence, we stand at a fork in the road. On one side lies redemption through suffering—but suffering nonetheless. This is the path of our nature as beings in the physical world. It winds its way according to trial and error in the cascade of circumstances that comprise one human life or many lifetimes, until inevitably we learn to recognize good and to choose it over evil, and we reach the state of fulfillment that is our destiny. The other path is that of the Zohar and Kabbalah: the path of spiritual transformation, and desire to receive for the sake of sharing. This, too, is not easy in the sense that we usually understand that word, but neither does it entail the suffering that the alternative path always includes. It requires certainty in the power of the kabbalistic tools and teachings, and diligence in using them, in order to reach our final goal of oneness with God. The Light of the Creator is present along both paths. They exist for the purpose of uniting human beings with the Creator, and it must be said once again that that purpose will ultimately be achieved.

In the preceding passages, the Zohar simply designates these two alternatives as "right" and "left." It is a fundamental kabbalistic teaching—perhaps *the* fundamental teaching—that when a sufficient number of people have chosen to use the divinely given spiritual tools, a critical mass will be achieved that will bring about the redemption of humanity as a whole, even including those who have followed the negative path. That, one might say, is the good news. The bad news is that the reverse is also true, as has been proven on a number of occasions in the biblical narrative. When evil has become sufficiently widespread, a general cleansing must take place, on a scale that transcends the virtue or depravity of individual human beings. At that point, the wheat is no longer separated from the chaff. Everything is considered chaff.

> The wicked people of the world go out of their way to attract the Angel of Darkness upon themselves. Therefore, because they give the Angel permission, he snatches their souls. But he never takes a soul without permission. That is why the verse above reads "has come before me." The Angel of Darkness comes before the Creator for permission to bring darkness upon the faces of the people of the world.

What kind of "permission" is referred to here? First, permission granted by the wicked themselves. Adam and Eve were not forced to eat the fruit of the forbidden tree. They were not even coerced.

They may have been misled as to the consequences of their actions, but like any good dissembler the serpent stayed as close to the truth as possible in everything he said. His power depended on the free will and the conscious decisions of anyone who chose to follow him. In short, there are no unwilling victims of the evil inclination. As someone (perhaps it was the serpent) once said, "You can't cheat an honest man."

But even more is required in order for the Angel of Darkness to do his work. He must also obtain the permission of the Creator— as in the book of Job, where the angel directly confronts God about the righteousness of a seemingly blameless person, and is granted the right to test him. According to kabbalistic teaching, a somewhat similar conversation between the Creator and the Angel of Darkness takes place once a year regarding every human being. At Rosh Hashanah, the New Year, the Angel presents an accounting of all our spiritual attainments and shortcomings and asks permission to intervene in our lives. If the Creator decides that judgment must be rendered, it is only because we have "asked for it" through the conduct of our lives.

Even then, there may still be a way out. The Angel of Darkness, for example, cannot take a person who is engaged in Torah study— which refers not only to the reading of sacred texts, but also "study" in the larger sense of living as a sharing human being. At the end of his life, King David was thus engaged from morning till night, and though his time had come to leave the world the Angel of Darkness was quite disarmed. It was only when David happened to stumble while walking that he took his mind off the teachings for an instant, and in that moment he was taken by death.

At the time of the Flood, the Creator warned Noah that he must prevent himself from being seen by the Angel:

If there is a plague in a city, or in the world, a person should not show himself in the marketplace, because the Angel of Darkness has received permission to destroy everything. That is why the Creator told Noah, "It behooves you to take heed and not show yourself before the Angel. It is because the Angel has permission that I told you to make an ark of gopher wood, so that he should have no power over you."

You may wonder how the ark survived. As long as a person's face is not seen by the Angel of Darkness, he cannot rule over him. We know this from Egypt, and the verse, "None of you shall go out the door of his house until morning." (Exodus 12:22) That is why Noah and all those who joined him hid within the ark, where the Angel had no power over them.

Throughout the Zohar, there is a profound recognition of life's tragic dimension. In the Zohar's pages there is no turning away from the fact that wicked people prosper, that good people suffer, and that innocent people die seemingly before their time. Side by side with this determination to face facts, the Zohar also intends to reveal the Creator as thoroughly just and loving. How can these two imperatives be reconciled? The only solution lies in our complete acceptance of responsibility for whatever befalls us, even when it seems beyond all understanding. The true kabbalist never sees himself as a victim. Though personally innocent of any overt wrongdoing, in not removing himself from danger or bad company he may nonetheless allow himself to be swept away by negative forces larger than himself, and in that event, he must accept responsibility wholeheartedly. If he dies in a plague, if he is exiled by a war, if his house burns down and his family is lost, there may be some apprehensible reason for this—or it could simply be a matter of his *tikkun*—something operative on a level beyond his perception that is offering him a chance for transformation. In any case, we must have certainty in the divine wisdom. In the words of Job: "Though He slay me, yet I will honor Him."

As the Zohar makes clear, the Flood was one of those instances of a negative critical mass.

Vol. 2, p. 361

Come and behold: Because the generation of Noah was stubborn and bold enough to sin openly, the Creator brought Judgment upon them. Rabbi Yitzchak said that if a person sins in secret, then the Creator is merciful. If the person repents, he is pardoned and forgiven. But if he does not repent his sins, the Creator reveals them for all to see.

In the same manner, the generation of the Flood was openly destroyed. How was this done? Scalding waters spurted up from the abyss, skinning them alive. As skin was torn from flesh, they were left only with their bones, and then the bones came asunder. As it is written: "And they were wiped from the face of the earth." (Genesis 7:23) This is similar to, "Let them be blotted out from the book of living." (Psalms 69:29) We learn from this that they shall not participate in the resurrection and will not rise in the Day of Judgment.

The kabbalists explain that when a human being dies and the body decomposes, a tiny bone at the base of the spine always remains intact. This bone, called the *luz,* is the seed from which the physical self will arise when humanity is redeemed and the dead are resurrected. But the generation of the Flood are excluded from this process. They are gone forever, and not even a tiny bone of them remains.

Vol. 2, pp. 387–390

The Creator wanted to protect Noah by hiding him out of sight, so that the impure Spirit could not destroy him. The words, "And Noah went in" mean that he entered the ark to be hidden from sight. The words, "because of the waters of the Flood" indicate that the waters actually pushed him into the ark. He saw the waters of the Flood and was afraid. As a result, he "went into the ark." And he protected himself by staying in the ark for 12 months. Why 12 months? On this point, Rabbi Yitzchak and Rabbi Yehuda had different opinions. One said that the 12 months are the period of the sentence of the wicked in Gehenom; the other said that the 12 months were to enable Noah to complete 12 stages of purification, so that he and all the others could emerge cleansed.

Rabbi Chiya quoted the verse, "A prudent man foresees evil and hides himself" (Proverbs 22:3), saying that this verse refers to Noah who entered the ark and hid himself in it. And he entered the ark only when the waters forced him to do so. Before he went into the ark, he saw the Angel of Darkness walking among the people and encircling them. Because Noah saw the Angel of Darkness, he entered the ark and hid. Thus, it is written: "A prudent man foresees evil and hides himself." "Foresees evil" refers to the Angel of Darkness, whom he saw on the waters of the Flood, and from whom he hid.

Rabbi Yosi explained that when death rages throughout the world, a wise man will hide and not appear in the open. This prevents the Angel of Darkness from seeing him, because when the Angel receives permission, he destroys everything in front of him and everyone who openly passes *before* him. A verse reads, ". . . but the simple pass on and are punished" (Proverbs 22:3), referring to those who pass in front of him, are seen by him, and therefore punished. Another explanation is that "pass on" means that those who transgress the commandments of their Master are therefore punished. Thus, a "prudent man foresees evil and hides himself" refers to Noah, while "the simple pass on and are punished" refers to the people of his generation.

One senses in these passages the Zohar's portrayal of Noah as a slightly compromised *tzaddik*—a great soul, to be sure, but not at the level of Moses or Abraham. Noah enters the ark out of prudence, or even fear: "down to earth" emotions as befits this "man of the ground," but not what we might expect of a great patriarch. However, as events after the Flood would demonstrate, Noah's troubles were only just beginning.

Vol. 2, p. 396

He hid himself in the ark and remained inside it. Later it is written, "And Elohim remembered Noah." Rabbi Shimon said: "Come and behold: while Judgment is executed, there is no remembrance. But after Judgment has been executed and the wicked have been removed from the world, then the word 'remember' is mentioned. When Judgment prevails in the world, there is no supernal mating above and the Angel of Darkness rages throughout the world below. Thus, there is no positive remembrance, for remembrance means mating."

Remembrance means mating? Kabbalah teaches that the real opposing forces in the world are chaos and order, fragmentation and unity. When negative energy predominates, there is separation where there needs to be connection. In the preceding paragraph, forgetting is presented as an aspect of disunity, and remembrance as an expression of intimate contact. Remembrance here means rekindling the Creator's Light in our lives, which the Zohar depicts not as an operation of the intellect, but quite frankly as an act of love.

CHAPTER 15

THE BINDING OF ISAAC

Genesis 22:1–2

> *And it came to pass after these things that the Creator tested Abraham and said to him, "Abraham," and he replied, "Behold, here I am." And the Creator said, "Take now your son, the one whom you love, Isaac, and go to the land of Moriah, and offer him there as a burnt offering at the place that I will show you."*

The events of Genesis 22 are some of the most difficult in the entire biblical narrative. If the Creator is the source of all benevolence, how could He call upon His most faithful servant to sacrifice his own son, whose very birth was nothing less than a miracle? The central problem of Abraham's life, and of his marriage with Sarah, was the pain of being without a child—and their greatest achievement was the resolution of that problem through trust in God. Now, it seems, the Creator Himself is calling for the destruction of what has been brought into being seemingly against all odds. Why would a loving God do such a thing?

Commentaries on this episode have set it in the context of a challenge to the Creator by the negative Angel. As in the book of Job, the Angel insists that Abraham is a righteous man only because he has gotten everything he wanted. What is more, he tells God, Abraham has never expressed sufficient gratitude. The Creator gave him a son, but he has never really given anything back. If God were to take away the material basis for Abraham's righteous behavior, he would turn out to be just another flawed being. So the Creator agreed to impose this test. While this may be a narrative explanation for Genesis 22, however, it is far from consoling to the lay reader. Is not God playing sadistic games with the lives of His most devoted believers?

The Zohar begins its discussion of the binding of Isaac with a reference to the encounter between the Creator and the Adversary:

Vol. 3, pp. 491–494

"And it came to pass after these things . . ." Rabbi Shimon said: "We have learned that the words 'And it came to pass (Heb. *vayehi*) in the days of' are said concerning trouble. Thus, even though it is not written 'in the days of,' there is still a certain tinge of distress, for it says, 'It came to pass that the Creator tested Abraham,' which means that the evil inclination came to lay accusations before the Creator."

The Adversary looks for openings. He is an opportunist, and if there are no opportunities he is powerless. And by revealing openings for negativity, he performs a valuable service. In this sense, the Adversary is like an attorney who aggressively defends a notorious criminal: He may seem to be acting reprehensibly, but he is really preserving the strength and integrity of the legal system as a whole.

Therefore, Kabbalah teaches, when the Adversary calls Abraham's virtue into question, he is, in effect, saying, "I see an opening here. Abraham is not yet complete. It is possible to raise doubts and questions about him, and it is my job to do that. What's more, if the doubts prove to be well founded, it is my job to create as much chaos as I can." The Adversary's actions should not be viewed as "malign." This is simply its nature, what it was created to do.

When the Creator agrees to test Abraham, it is by no means a capricious decision. The purpose is not just to see what will happen, but to bring about the final completion of Abraham's soul. The intention is not to bring down a faithful servant, but to elevate him beyond any possible accusation.

Abraham, of course, has already passed many tests. This final one will be the most difficult, for it calls upon him to act wholly against his nature. As we saw in chapter 6, Abraham is a pure embodiment of kindness and generosity. In kabbalistic terminology, his connection is with the *Sefirah* of *Chesed*. The energy of judgment and severity associated with the *Sefirah* of *Gvurah* is foreign to him—and that is precisely what the Adversary has revealed as an opening. As the foundation of the spiritual circuitry that must be flawlessly constructed if the redemption of humanity is ever to be realized, Abraham must be made a complete soul. That is the purpose of this last trial, as the Zohar makes clear.

There was no judgment in Abraham previously. He had consisted entirely of kindness (Heb. *Chesed*). Now water was mixed with fire; kindness was mixed with judgment (Heb. *Gvurah*). Abraham did not achieve perfection until he prepared himself to execute judgment and establish it in its place.

So all his life, he did not reach perfection until now, until water mixed with fire and fire with water—right with left and left with right. This is why it is written "The Creator tested Abraham" and not "tested Isaac." Because the Creator invited Abraham to be included with judgment. When Abraham performed the act of binding Isaac, the fire entered the water, that is, judgment entered kindness, and they were perfected by one another.

This is what the act of judgment accomplished: It included one within the other. This is also the reason why the Adversary came and accused Abraham of not being properly perfected until he performed the act of judgment by binding Isaac.

But Abraham's spiritual completion is only part of what takes place in Genesis 22. Secular interpretations of this episode usually depict Abraham preparing to sacrifice a young boy. But the Zohar points out that this was not the case. Isaac was a grown man, and his participation was an act of free choice equal to that of Abraham. Moreover, Kabbalah associates Isaac with the reciprocal of Abraham's spiritual essence. It was Abraham's nature to give to others, and it was Isaac's nature to receive. Kabbalistically, this does not make Isaac a "bad" person. He was like Abraham in that he had not yet achieved the completion of his soul, but he was the opposite of Abraham in what he lacked to reach that completion. Allowing himself to become an offering to God went against Isaac's essence, which was connected to the *Sefirah* of *Gvurah*—that is, the energy of assertion, judgment, and desire for oneself. Once this is recognized, the binding of Isaac becomes something very different from conventional interpretations. It is no longer a story of child abuse that makes us uncomfortable with the Bible. Instead, it is an act of collaboration between two people who are aware that their actions are of supreme importance, as evidenced by the fact that those actions are supremely difficult.

The phrase "tested Abraham" should be studied carefully. Perhaps it should have been written, "tested Isaac," because Isaac was already 37 years old and his father could no longer be punished for his sins. So if Isaac had said, "I refuse to obey," his father would not have been punished because of him.

Come and behold this mystery. Isaac was crowned in his place together with Abraham, and the fire combined with the water and rose upward. Abraham with kindness rose up, and Isaac with judgment rose up. Then the issue was settled properly, as fire and water made peace between one another, were reconciled and combined, and became inclusive of each other.

The "miracle" of this story is the commitment of the protagonists to transcend the limits of their own contrasting natures. Kabbalah teaches that as Abraham walked with Isaac to the place of sacrifice, Abraham was granted a clear vision of his future grandson Jacob, the son of Isaac. How was Abraham to understand this? Was the vision of Jacob a glimpse of what was about to be lost? Perhaps the vision was telling him that he must rebel and refuse to perform the sacrifice, lest Jacob never be born. Or had the vision been sent to reassure Abraham that the sacrifice would not need to be completed after all? The kabbalists tell us that Abraham really did not know what lay in store. Though he was aware of the crucial role that had been ordained for Jacob in the spiritual destiny of humanity, he was fully prepared to carry out the offering of Isaac. He had full trust in the Creator—not just that the outcome would necessarily be what he wanted as an individual human being, but that it would be in accord with the best interests of all humanity, and even of all Creation.

Genesis 22:9–12

They arrived at the place of which the Creator had told them. Abraham built an altar there. He arranged the wood, bound his son

Isaac, and laid him on top of the wood. Abraham picked up the knife to slay his son. Then an angel called to him from heaven: "Abraham! Abraham!" And he answered, "Here I am." And he said, "Do not raise your hand against the boy, or do anything to harm him. For now I know that you fear God, since you have not withheld your son from me."

This biblical passage recalls the one quoted at the beginning of this chapter, in which the Creator first calls on Abraham to offer his son. But there is an important difference. Here Abraham's name is spoken twice, signifying first the person he was, and then the new level of spiritual elevation he has achieved. His transformation—and that of Isaac—from their respective identifications with *Chesed* and *Gvurah* would later be manifest in the person of Jacob, the embodiment of the *Sefirah* of *Tiferet,* expressing synthesis, balance, and harmony. Jacob would be the next step in the construction of the system that now connects us with the Creator, and that ultimately will bring us unity with Him.

The double utterance of Abraham's name suggests another duality in these verses. We are told that an angel is speaking, and some commentators have understood this to be the angel who, in Genesis 18, declared to Abraham that he would "return when life is due"—that is, when Isaac's life needed to be saved. On the other hand, there was also an inference in Genesis 18 that the angel was really (or also) the Creator Himself. Here the ambiguity is even stronger: Somewhere between the middle of the last sentence and its end, "God" becomes "me."

Regarding that sentence, we should understand by now that when the Bible or the Zohar refer to "fear" of God, this is something very different from fear as we ordinarily use the word. In this context, Abraham's fearing the Creator simply recognizes Abraham's connection with the aspect of God that expresses itself through judgment. It is the Creator's acknowledgment of the completion of Abraham's soul.

As it does so often, the Zohar sums up this most controversial biblical episode in the context of what today might be called family dynamics:

> Who has never seen a merciful father do a cruel thing to his son? It is only to settle the dispute and combine water with fire, and each one is properly crowned in its place. And this remained so until Jacob appeared, who was the expression of balance and harmony between them (Heb. *Tiferet*). Then, everything was properly established, and all three Patriarchs achieved perfection.

Although this story is often referred to as the "sacrifice" of Isaac, Kabbalah (and all midrashic commentaries) substitute the word *akedah* (Heb. *binding*). In the literal narrative, it is Isaac who is bound with ropes by his father. But more significantly, both Isaac and Abraham succeed in binding the limiting, reflexive aspects of their natures, and thereby enable themselves to reach a new level of being. What is really sacrificed in this story is nothing other than the characters' former selves.

From a literary point of view, it is clear the *akedah* episode is rich in irony and allegory. But reading the Zohar should never be just an exercise in connoisseurship. This story connects us with the souls of Abraham and Isaac in a very literal way—not only intellectually, but through the Light of the Creator that Kabbalah describes as the true foundation of our being. We can draw strength from this connection whenever we need to make a painful sacrifice in our own lives. We can gain certainty that the binding of self-serving desire will ultimately set us free.

CHAPTER 16

JACOB AND ESAU

The great twentieth-century kabbalist Rabbi Yehuda Ashlag told of a powerful king who, in his old age, became the father of a son. The king loved the child beyond all telling, and from the day of the boy's birth his well-being was the most important concern in the land. Great teachers were brought from all over the world to provide for the education of the prince. Musicians and artists created splendid works for his enjoyment. Chefs cooked magnificent meals for him every night.

Yet the child cared nothing for all of this. Simply put, he was a fool. He was oblivious to the works of art. He had no appreciation for the carefully prepared feasts. Learning held no attraction for him. Needless to say, this caused the king great distress. Despite his position, power, and wealth, his life no longer held any meaning.

A great disappointment such as the king experienced can befall anyone, even the most powerful people in the world, and indeed it has happened often enough. But Rabbi Ashlag used the story to illustrate something that cannot happen, and to clarify an important difference between power in the physical world and the ultimate dominion of the Creator. We are the children of God, and He loves us beyond imagining, but we can never disappoint him in the sense that human children can break the hearts of their parents. We will all fulfill God's true intention. Kabbalah teaches that every one of us will someday be a *tzaddik*.

Until that day comes, we will meet many twists and turns in the road. The pulls of positive and negative forces are not distributed equally among human beings, nor is the ability of individuals even to recognize the difference between good and evil. These issues are powerfully dramatized in the portrayal of Jacob and Esau in the book of Genesis. Theirs is one of the most complex stories in the biblical narrative, and one that requires even more attention than usual to what is implied but not explicitly said. It lends itself especially well, therefore, to the Zohar's style of discursive analysis.

Even at first reading, we may come to the story of Jacob and Esau with a number of preconceptions. We know beforehand that Jacob is one of the biblical patriarchs: The Creator Himself speaks of "Abraham, Isaac, and Jacob." We may be aware also that Jacob's twin brother, Esau, is one of the Bible's villains. Yet what actually happens in the tale may lead us to question those assumptions.

What, after all, is really so bad about Esau? Yes, he was born a reddish color, and covered with hair, but today we are disinclined to condemn people based on their physical characteristics at birth. He grows up to be a "man of the outdoors," which is also by no means a bad thing. He is very close to his father, and even the rabbinical commentaries agree that no one has ever exceeded Esau's degree of filial loyalty. Most puzzling of all, the famous incident of Genesis 25, in which Esau trades his birthright to Jacob for a bowl of lentil stew, seems to be an instance of pure manipulation. Esau "spurns" his birthright, the Bible tells us, but who among us has not made an ill-considered decision at one time or another? And what is a birthright, anyway?

As with Abraham, however, there is an extensive personal history present in the Bible, in an encrypted form. The color red, for example, beyond its obvious connotations of blood and violence, is associated in Kabbalah with the desire to receive for the self alone. Colors, like so much else, are encoded in the biblical text just as they are in the world itself. The discovery that blood consists of red and white cells came as no surprise to kabbalists. Blood, the link between soul and body, must embody both the red and the white, both the energy of giving and that of receiving. Red cells manifest the desire for nourishment and growth; white cells, whose function is to destroy infection, are created to give of themselves.

When Esau asks for the stew, the midrash commentaries point out that lentils are red, and that Esau responded to the color with a animal lust that made the food irresistible. The generally more elegant prose of biblical translations does not convey the flavor, so to speak, of the Hebrew original, in which Esau says something like, "Pour some of that red stuff down my throat." And did Jacob know that his brother would react this way? Was he preparing that red stew because he knew Esau would be hungry when he came in from the fields?

If Esau is portrayed as driven by instinct and animal desire, perhaps Jacob can be construed as guileful and calculating. But here an extremely important principle comes into play. Although it is easy to see how Jacob can be taken for a dissembler, it was actually Esau who was known for slyness and cunning. Midrash tell how as a youth Esau connived to fool Isaac into thinking he was a diligent student of the sacred writings. Though he spent his time in the fields trapping animals, he would hear a phrase of Torah now and then, which he then solemnly repeated to his father, as if he had been pondering it all day. Later, it is said that he took many pagans as his wives, keeping this from Isaac as well.

To compound the problem, it may be that Isaac was not even completely fooled. For one thing, he liked the meat that Esau brought home from his hunting excursions. And he also had a certain affinity with the negative aspects of Esau's nature. Both Isaac and Esau, Kabbalah teaches, were connected to Left-Column energy of *Gvurah*, severity or judgment. Yet there were also basic differences between these two men. Isaac was a channel for the desire to receive, but the purity of his nature was such that this expressed itself as desire to receive for the sake of drawing Light—something very different from Esau's desire to receive for the self.

The greatness of Jacob derived from his balance of Right- and Left-Column forces, and his association with the Central-Column *Sefirah* of *Tiferet*, or balance. Another very important kabbalistic teaching about Jacob identifies him as a reincarnation of Adam. As will become clear, this transmigration of Adam's soul answers many questions often raised by lay readers concerning Jacob and his conduct in Genesis 25.

So before we even look closely at the biblical incidents and the Zohar's commentary (which follows), we can already say that Esau is a kind of primitive personality, closer to the animal kingdom than to the world of men, much less the Upper World of the spirit. Yet he is by no means without intelligence. He knows how to manipulate others, and even himself. A wild, unevolved personality such as Esau's develops an obvious service to its own negative traits. Such a person comes to express those traits without any hesitation, embarrassment, or limit—in Esau's case, openly stealing and killing at any opportunity. In today's context he might be a very successful, if unscrupulous businessman, ruthless and opportunistic. In fact, even in the Bible he is portrayed as a successful businessman in as much as, although he trades away his birthright, he somehow has become wealthy by the time of his reunion with Jacob in Genesis 33. Jacob, meanwhile, has been tricked into many years of servitude for the idol-worshipping Laban!

Any lingering impression of Jacob, therefore, as a deceitful individual is clearly mistaken from a kabbalistic viewpoint. Jacob was going beyond his nature, doing whatever was necessary in a positive way to ensure that the way of the desire to receive for the sake of sharing would be the system by which the world operated and drew Light. He was being cunning, which was not really his nature, in order to save the world. And all the while he was worried that he would not be spiritually strong enough to live up to this challenge.

If he tricked Esau out of his birthright, we are to understand that he himself had been tricked by his brother many times in the past. Moreover, in the important deception perpetrated on Isaac, when Jacob disguised himself as Esau in order to gain his father's blessing, it was his mother Rebecca who initiated the idea.

When Isaac asked Esau to bring him some venison to eat in exchange for his blessing, Rebecca, knowing that Esau would simply go steal someone's domestic animal and slaughter it, suggested that Jacob disguise himself and take Esau's place. Jacob was reluctant to do so and even wept at the prospect of being found out. But Rebecca assured him that if there were any blame attached to the deception, she would take it upon herself, both with Isaac and in the Upper World. In any case, Rebecca knew that divine law was on her side: When something sacred is liable to fall into the possession of those not worthy of it, we have not only the right but also the obligation to prevent that from happening. This is the case with Isaac's blessing. Rebecca knew that Jacob was a *tzaddik* and that Esau was a manifestation of the desire to receive for the self alone. She was determined to use any means necessary to keep Isaac's blessing from Esau.

The Zohar begins the discussion of this episode as follows.

Vol. 4, pp. 250–262

Isaac said to Esau "and go out to the field, and catch me some venison." (Genesis 27:3) And Esau went hunting in order to be blessed by Isaac, who said to him, "and I will bless you before God." It would have been as well just to say, "and I will bless you," but since he added "before God," the throne of glory of the Creator then trembled and said: Could it be, that the serpent is freed from curses, and Jacob remains subject to them?

At that time [the angel] Michael came before Jacob with the Shechinah. Isaac knew that and saw that the Garden of Eden was with Jacob, so he blessed him. When Esau entered, Gehenom entered with him. Therefore: "And Isaac trembled very much" (Genesis 27:33) because he had previously thought that Esau was not of that side. Therefore he said, "and I have blessed him. Moreover, he shall remain blessed."

There are some surprising revelations in these passages. To understand them, we must be aware of the teaching that Jacob was Adam reincarnated—and that the blessing of Isaac had the power to reverse the judgment imposed on humans at the time of the sin. Clearly, this was a very important moment. The possibility that the blessing might be given to the wrong person—much less someone connected to the negative side, such as Esau—was disturbing even to the Creator. Such an occurrence would release the serpent from judgment while humanity would remain subject to it.

The Zohar gives us a glimpse inside Isaac's confused state of mind. His eyes were very weak. Some midrashic commentaries interpret his weakened vision as punishment for his making his blessing conditional on Esau's providing him with venison. Other commentaries suggest that the Creator had blinded Isaac to further the deception by Rebecca and Jacob. But as the Zohar makes clear, Isaac was not even fooled, at least not completely. Rebecca had told Jacob to wear Esau's special hunting garments, but when Jacob came near his father the garments had miraculously acquired the floral aroma of the Garden of Eden itself. On a spiritual level, this was because the curse that had accompanied the expulsion from Eden was about to be lifted. But it was very worrisome to Isaac. The scent told him he was in the presence of a *tzaddik*.

But by this time a process was under way on a scale larger even than the personal interaction between two patriarchs. It was another occasion, like the building of the ark by Noah or the giving of the Law by Moses, in which the spiritual circuitry of all creation was about to change.

Continuing to present justification for Jacob's deception, the Zohar describes it as just recompense for the serpent's lying to Adam. And the ploy masterminded by Rebecca was effective. Isaac gave Jacob his blessing.

Genesis 27:28

Isaac said to him, "Come near me, and kiss me, my son." And he came near and kissed him: and he smelled the smell of his clothing, and blessed him, and said, "see, the smell of my son is as the smell of the field that the Creator has blessed. Therefore God give you the dew of heaven, and the fatness of the earth, and corn and wine; let people serve you, and nations bow down to you; be lord over your brethren, and let your mother's sons bow down to you; cursed be everyone that curses you, and blessed be he that blesses you."

For that reason Jacob behaved with cunning and guile, and brought blessings on Jacob, who resembled Adam, that were taken from the serpent of the lying lips, who talked and acted deceitfully, in order to incite Adam to sin and to bring curses upon the world. For that reason, Jacob behaved with cunning and misled his father, so as to bring blessings upon the world and to snatch from the serpent what he had withheld. This was measure for measure, of which it is written, "For he loved cursing, and it came to him: and he delighted not in blessings, and it was far from him." (Psalms 109:17) Concerning the serpent, the verse reads, "You are cursed above all cattle, and above every beast of the field." (Genesis 3:14) He stayed accursed forever more, and Jacob came and took the blessings.

It would be reasonable to infer from this story that in deceiving his father, cheating his brother, Jacob was a less than spiritual person. But this would be an overly simplistic and moralistic conclusion. This story is actually about using whatever means were necessary to create the metaphysical system of our universe. In fact, rather than being the mere usurper of his brother's birthright, Jacob was actually the restorer of the birthright of humankind. In borrowing the methods of the serpent, Jacob was fighting fire with fire; what had been taken with trickery could only be retrieved with trickery. Kabbalah teaches that the cause is always hidden so what we perceive are only effects. Therefore, as we cannot know all the reasons for another person's actions we must withhold judgment. It is not for us to say whether someone is a good person or an evil person. Behavior we might deem evil might have a righteous purpose behind it as in the story of David and Batsheva, or in the case of Jacob, who in his seeming guile was only acting "measure for measure" with the serpent in order to retrieve Light back from an impure system.

From the time of Adam, Jacob was destined to take from the serpent all these blessings, and the serpent was to remain accursed, never to be released from them. For the serpent deceived Adam and his wife and brought evil on him and the world. Then came Jacob, who took the blessings that were his own. Esau harbored hatred toward Jacob on account of the blessings, as it is written, "and Esau hated Jacob because of the blessing." (Genesis 27:41)

Of the time when the serpent brought curses upon the world, and the land was accursed, it is written, "And to the man he said: Because you have hearkened to the voice of your wife . . . cursed is the ground for your sake" (Genesis 3:17), for it will not produce fruit nor vegetation in proper measure. To rescind this judgment, Jacob was given blessings for the time after the advent of Mashiach. ". . . and the fatness of the earth" means that the earth will be whole again, contravening the curse, "in sorrow shall you eat of it." "Of the dew of heaven" refers to the curse, "thorns and thistles shall it bring forth to you." In opposition to the curse, "In the sweat of your face shall you eat bread," he was blessed as it is written, "let peoples serve you, and nations bow down to you." They will cultivate the land and till the field, as it is written, "and the sons of the alien shall be your plowmen and your vine dressers." (Isaiah 61:5) Jacob took it all measure for measure, each blessing corresponding to one curse of the Tree of Knowledge. The Creator caused Jacob to receive these blessings and cleave to his place and portion, while Esau cleaved to his own place and portion.

When Isaac had finished blessing Jacob, according to the biblical text, and not long after Jacob had left the presence of his father, Esau came in from his hunting. And he also had made savory food.

He brought it to Isaac and said, "Let my father arise, and eat of his son's venison, that your soul may bless me." (Genesis 27:30)

But, of course, the blessing had already been given. Esau cried out in pain—and he demanded that his father give him whatever beneficence he might have withheld. Isaac complied as best he could: "Behold, your dwelling shall be the fatness of the earth, and the dew of heaven from above; and by your sword shall you live, and shall serve your brother; and it shall come to pass when you shall have the dominion, that you shall break his yoke from off your neck."

The Zohar interprets Esau's worldly prosperity as a manifestation of Isaac's blessing. Esau will receive his gifts here in the physical realm, within the confines of time and space. Jacob's blessing will be eternal and will not be constrained by the boundaries of finite existence—but its full manifestation must await the arrival of *Mashiach* (the Messiah) and the final transformation of mankind.

> Rabbi Chizkiyah said: "We see that the fatness of the earth and the dew of heaven were the blessing Esau later received, as it is written, 'of the fatness of the earth, and of the dew of heaven from above.' "(Genesis 27:39) Rabbi Shimon said: "The one is not like the other. The blessing of Esau does not resemble the blessing of Jacob. It is written of Jacob, 'of the dew of heaven, and the fatness of the earth,' and of Esau, 'of the fatness of the earth, and of the dew of heaven,' with earth preceding heaven, for there is no resemblance between them."

In other words, depending on which brother received his father's blessing, a very different spiritual system would prevail in our universe. Were Esau to have received the blessing, desire to receive for the self alone would have ruled the day. But for Jacob to receive it meant that consciousness would take precedence over matter—that desire to receive in order to share would draw the Light of the Creator into our lives.

> Also, Jacob was blessed above and below, and Esau only below. And though it is written, "and it shall come to pass when you shall have the dominion, that you shall break his yoke from off your neck" (Genesis 27:40), this was concerning this world, but up above, nothing is canceled, as it is written, "For God's portion is his people: Jacob is the lot of His inheritance." (Deuteronomy 32:9) Come and behold: When Jacob and Esau started to avail themselves of the blessings, Jacob received his share from above, and Esau took his share below.

To say that "Jacob was blessed [both] above and below" signifies that when the blessing originates from above (the Light) material blessings may attend the spiritual blessing. But such is not the case when the blessing originates in the material world. Because they have no spiritual basis, such blessings will be entirely transitory.

> Rabbi Yosi, the son of Rabbi Shimon, son of Lakunia, asked Rabbi Elazar: "Has your father explained why the blessings with which Isaac blessed Jacob did not prevail, while the blessings Isaac bestowed on Esau all did?"
> He replied that all these blessings prevailed, along with other blessings that the Creator gave to Jacob. But

at first, Jacob received his blessings above only. And Esau received below. When Mashiach will arise, Jacob will receive above and below, and Esau will lose everything. He will have no portion and inheritance or remembrance in the world. This is the meaning of the verse, "And the house of Jacob shall be fire, and the house of Joseph flame, and the house of Esau for stubble" (Obadiah 1:8), for Esau will lose everything, and Jacob will inherit both worlds, this world and the world to come.

Esau's blessings were not lasting because he did nothing to earn them. Without real spiritual work, transformation cannot take place; we do not cleave to the Light. Although this is the material plane, all we receive is earned by our spiritual work. And that which is not earned, is simply lost.

Here the Zohar tells us that initially Jacob saw only spiritual blessings; Esau only material. But at the coming of the Messiah, those who have been "blessed from below" will lose everything, whereas Jacob—who symbolically stands for those who have earned their blessings through the spiritual order of things—will "inherit the earth," so to speak. Even now the spiritual reality is the only true reality, but currently we still labor under the material illusion. If we are able to understand that material blessings are illusory and strive instead to earn spiritual blessings like Jacob, then we will receive the true blessing of God.

Of that time, it is written, "And liberators shall ascend upon mount Zion to judge the mountain of Esau; and the kingdom shall be God's." The kingdom that Esau received in this world shall be for the Creator alone.

Although the Creator has dominion above and below, He lets other peoples rule, giving each a part and inheritance in this world for their use. At the time of Mashiach He will take the kingdoms from them all, and it will be solely His, as it is written, "And the Creator shall be King over all the earth: on that day the Creator shall be one, and His name One" (Zechariah 14:9).

Concerning the verse, "And Jacob was scarce gone out," Rabbi Shimon said: "This refers to two goings out: those of the Shechinah and of Jacob. When Jacob entered, the Shechinah entered with him. Isaac said the blessings and the Shechinah approved. Therefore, when Jacob went out, the Shechinah went out with him."

From a kabbalistic viewpoint, we should not think of Esau as someone who is guilty of sinful actions, but as a symbol of a selfish desire to receive. His primary concern was satisfying his immediate physical needs, rather than participating in the ongoing project of Creation. In today's vernacular, he "thought small." He abandoned the greater good in order to satisfy a craving that had overwhelmed him.

This shortsighted, reflexive behavior is the essence of the desire to receive for ourselves. The negative inclination has no sense of proportion or relative value. It reacts to temptation or opportunity like a cat to catnip. In line with this, on the Sabbath we traditionally set aside a tiny piece of bread for the Angel of Darkness, who will become completely preoccupied with even this inconsequential sop. Why is the other side happy with such a small piece, when there is still the whole loaf to eat? That is simply the nature of the desire to receive. It becomes obsessed with whatever satisfies its desire *right now*. So the teaching here is not that Esau is guilty in a moral sense; his is simply a robotic consciousness, no more elevated than an insect's.

Conversely, we should understand Jacob's apparently calculating behavior as an expression of a higher purpose. He knows that he is on a spiritual mission beyond his individual needs: By receiving Isaac's blessing, he can rescind the judgment that befell Adam in the Garden of Eden. The moment of the blessing was a turning point in the history of Creation. Had Jacob not been spiritually strong enough to receive and hold the blessing, and had Esau taken it instead, the world would be dominated by the desire to receive for the self alone. Had that happened, Kabbalah teaches that a cleansing such as occurred at the time of Noah would have taken place, but this time the world would have been destroyed.

It is also important that Isaac did not know the identity of the person to whom he was giving the blessing. Though he was a patriarch, Isaac's consciousness was limited. Had he been aware of the complexities that were in play at the time of the blessing, his own limitations would have been built into the blessing itself. A similar principle is at work during the celebration of Purim. It is traditional to drink heavily on that occasion, in order to tap into an intensity of Light that can be reached only by erasing the inhibitions of our everyday consciousness.

> "Esau his brother came in from his hunting." Why is it written "his hunting," and not "the hunting"? It is because Esau's hunting contains no blessing. And the holy spirit cried out, "Do not eat the bread of him who has an evil eye." (Proverbs 23:6)
>
> "And he also had made savory food . . . Let my father arise." (Genesis 27:31) His speech was impertinent,

rough, and impolite. Come and behold the difference between Jacob and Esau. Jacob spoke to his father with humility. It is written, "And he came to his Isaac, and said, 'My father . . .'" Jacob did not want to frighten him, saying "Arise, I pray you, sit and eat of my venison." Esau, however, said, "Let my father arise."

Come and behold: When Esau entered, Gehenom came with him, and Isaac trembled with fear, as it is written, "And Isaac trembled very much." (Genesis 27:33) Why is "very much" used to describe "trembled"? Because Isaac never felt such fear and terror during his life. Even when he was strapped upon the altar and saw the knife, he did not tremble as when Esau entered and brought Gehenom with him. Then he said: "before you came, I blessed him. Moreover, he shall remain blessed." For I saw the Shechinah approving those blessings.

There is another explanation: When Isaac said, "I blessed him," a voice came forth, saying, "Moreover, he shall remain blessed." Isaac wanted to curse Jacob, but the Creator said to him, "It is you whom you curse, for you have said to him 'cursed be those that curse you, and blessed be those that bless you.'" (Genesis 27:29)

Isaac has been outsmarted, or has outsmarted himself. Even when it seems to him that he has been manipulated by Jacob and Rebecca, he cannot express his anger. As the Zohar explains, Isaac decreed a curse on anyone who harbored ill will toward Jacob, including Isaac himself. Or perhaps it was the Creator who added that very important codicil. But what these Zohar passages really communicate is a theme that is an essential kabbalistic theme: the order of precedence that obtains in the building of the spiritual structure, and the need to observe that order beyond the exigencies of circumstance or personality. The alternative, as we have observed several times, is not so much evil as it is chaos. The Zohar develops this theme further in its discussion of Jacob's marriages—first to Leah, and a week later to her sister Rachel.

CHAPTER 17

JACOB AND RACHEL

From a purely literary point of view, the biblical account of Rachel and Jacob is a great love story. From a spiritual standpoint, it is a powerful expression of the intimate connection between ourselves in the physical realm of creation and the Shechinahas, the divine presence called. Both these interpretations are correct, but kabbalistically the second represents a deeper and more enlightened understanding. With respect to our own lives, Kabbalah tells us that physical love is wonderful, but it is not an end in itself. It is, however, a stepping-stone to love for the Creator, for to truly love includes loving the God within and through that person.

Love is the supreme opportunity to fulfill our life's purpose of transformation—yet the experience of true love on earth also means that to a certain extent our purpose has already been fulfilled. Real love transcends ego needs. Of all the billions of people in the world, there are times when it seems as if there is only one for us. Kabbalah teaches that when the experience of unconditional love is genuine, it naturally extends itself to include all of Creation. Thus, through love for his wife, a man gains connection with the Shechinah, and by loving and understanding her husband, a woman can receive the male aspect of the Creator that infuses this world with the Light of fulfillment.

Genesis 29:1–5

Then Jacob went on his journey, and came into the land of the people of the east. And he looked, and behold, a well in the field, and lo, there were three flocks of sheep lying by it; for out of that well they watered their flocks; and a great stone was upon the well's mouth . . . and they rolled the stone from the well's mouth, and watered the sheep, and put the stone again upon the well's mouth in his place. . . . And Jacob said to them, "Do you know Laban the son of Nahor?" And they said, "We know him."

Vol. 5, pp. 82–85

Come and behold: Jacob was under the Holy Government in the land of Israel. After he left the land, he came under another dominion which was not holy. Before he came under that other dominion, the Creator was revealed to him in a dream. He saw what he saw, and the holy angels walked with him until he sat upon the well. After he sat on the well, the water rose toward him. So it was with Moshe because there his wife chanced to meet him. The secret of the well is that it only rises when it sees its union, that is, its spouse.

Jacob thought: I want to take a wife, to join the Shechinah, the secret of the well. My father, when he was to be married, sent a servant to find a source of water where a wife chanced to be found. But in Charan, where he was, Jacob did not find a well of water. Immediately, therefore, "Jacob lifted up his feet, and went to the land of the people of the east," where he chanced upon the well and met his wife.

A well, like a woman, is a source of life. Jacob's search for a mate reprises that of his father, yet it had a special character of its own. Isaac had instructed Jacob to marry a daughter of Laban, a wealthy idol worshipper of Charan who was also Jacob's uncle, and miracles had attended his traveling to that country. Time was foreshortened, so that he arrived the same day he departed his home, and when he arrived at the well he easily rolled the stone away by himself, though it usually required the combined efforts of all the shepherds. Then the well overflowed, and just at that moment the beautiful Rachel appeared, leading her father's sheep. It was the Creator who had sent her. She was to be Jacob's wife, though the course of their marriage would not be as easy as its beginning.

Laban was a swindler, and in fact he had been eagerly awaiting Jacob's arrival. Since he knew that Jacob's family was wealthy he was certain that Jacob had brought many gifts, just as long ago Isaac had brought gifts from his father Abraham when Isaac came to marry Rebecca. But Jacob had nothing.

Though disappointed, Laban decided he would rather marry his daughter off to a relative than to a stranger. But in order to take Rachel as his bride, Jacob had to agree to serve Laban for seven years. And he agreed to do so, despite the fact that he was anxious to start a family. The Creator, he knew, had ordained that twelve tribes would be born to him—and he was already eighty-four years old!

Laban was well known as a crook in Charan, and the "bait-and-switch" tactic used on Jacob was worthy of a seasoned con man. After serving Laban for seven years, Jacob's wedding to Rachel finally took place, but it was Rachel's sister Leah who was hidden under the bridal veil. Jacob did not realize the deception until the next morning, after he had consummated his marriage to Leah.

Rabbi Elazar mused that if a wife chanced to Jacob by the well, why was it not Leah? She gave many tribes to Jacob. But the Creator did not want to unite her with Jacob openly, as it is written: "And it came to pass, that in the morning, behold, it was Leah," (Genesis 29:25) but this was not revealed earlier.

Rachel's beauty would catch the eye and heart of Jacob, so he would establish his dwelling there. Because of her, Leah too was united with him. How did Jacob recognize Rachel? The shepherds told him, as it is written: "and behold, Rachel his daughter comes with the sheep." (Genesis 29:6)

A conventional reading of the hoax perpetrated on Jacob depicts him as a victim, and the perpetrators of the plot as thoroughly corrupt. The perpetrators, in fact, included Rachel herself, who informed Leah of a secret password Jacob had given her to guard against exactly this sort of deception. Moreover, it was the will of the Creator that Leah marry Jacob and become the mother of many tribes of Israel. The Bible describes Rachel as beautiful, while Leah is said to have "weak eyes." The midrash tells us that her eyes were damaged by incessant weeping. She longed to marry a *tzaddik*, yet her father had already betrothed her to none other than Esau himself. Now, with Rachel's complicity, she got her wish. The fact that this also served the interests of the dishonest Laban is irrelevant in terms of the bigger picture, which is always the focus of Kabbalah. Laban is pleased when Jacob agrees to serve him for another seven years in order to make Rachel his wife as well, but this is of no consequence from a spiritual perspective. The Bible itself makes this point: Jacob's fourteen years of service seemed to him "like only a few days" (Genesis 29:20), for at the spiritual level time is reckoned as perceived duration, not by the motion of a clock.

Nonetheless, it was a complicated situation, not only in the events themselves but in what transpired in the minds of the protagonists. Jacob thought of Rachel while he was making love with Leah, and this cost their firstborn son, Reuven, his patrimony:

Vol. 5, pp. 113–116

Woe to him who, because of that contemplation, is uprooted from the Tree of Life and attached to the Tree of Death, which has no branches. He who clings to it never sees goodness. He is without moisture, his fruits as bitter as wormwood. Of him it is said: "For he shall be like the juniper tree in the desert, and shall not see when good comes." (Jeremiah 17·6)

But good contemplation ascends and seizes the Tree of Life, embracing its branches and eating its fruits. All that is holy and all blessings come from it. He inherits life for his soul and healing for himself. Of him it is said: "For he shall be like a tree planted by the waters, and that spreads out its roots by the river. . . ."

Unaware that Leah was beside him in the marriage bed, Jacob quite naturally thought of Rachel, since it was Rachel whom he believed he had just married. As Benjamin Franklin wrote, "In the dark all cats are gray." Yet Kabbalah teaches that disconnection between thought and action always has an effect, especially in sexuality.

Every act in the world follows thought and contemplation. Concerning this, the scripture reads: "You shall therefore sanctify yourselves, and you shall be holy" (Exodus 11:44), because the sanctities of the world are manifested and drawn by means of good contemplation.

He who is defiled by the evil contemplation of thinking about another woman while inseminating his wife causes confusion in the Upper Worlds. As his thoughts change from his wife to another woman, so he causes change above. The body of the son he begets is called a "changed son," and his soul is also called "changed," for his thoughts were not drawn from holiness.

Yet it was revealed before the Creator that all Jacob did was true, and that he harbored thoughts of Truth. The night he had intercourse with Leah, his thoughts were of Rachel. He was with Leah and thought of Rachel, and his issue came from that thought.

Unknowingly he did this, because he did not know it was Leah. It was known before the Creator that Jacob's thought was not intentional and that Jacob wished to contemplate the way of Truth. Thus, his son Reuven was not disqualified as a member of the holy tribes.

Because thought is so important and translates into action, the Creator, who knew the place to which that contemplation clung during the insemination of the first drop, kept the birthright from Reuven, as it is written: "for he was the firstborn; but since he defiled his father's bed, his birthright was given to Joseph." (I Chronicles 5:1) The birthright was taken from Reuven and given to the place Jacob thought of. He thought of Rachel, and the desire clung to her; thus, the birthright was attached to Rachel.

Sometimes the connection between thought and sexuality can serve a noble purpose, as when the brother of a deceased husband marries the widow. Through the thoughts and desires of the surviving couple, the dead man literally becomes the child, and his line continues into the succeeding generation.

> In the same manner, contemplation and thought result in deeds drawn from that to which a man secretly attaches himself, as it is written: "the wife of the dead shall not marry abroad to a stranger: her husband's brother shall go in to her" (Deuteronomy 25:5). Here, his thought and desire should cleave to the soul of his dead brother. By that desire and thought he draws, he does his duty, so that the dead man's name shall not be erased from the world.
>
> This is the secret of the verse: "If he set his heart upon man, if he gather to himself his spirit and his breath." (Job 34:14) Assuredly this is so. Therefore in prayer, we need to desire, and also to contemplate upon it.

The Zohar represents the Creator as scrupulously balanced in his evaluation of Jacob's circumstances. On the one hand, Jacob had been thinking of one woman while making love to another. Therefore the birthright that should belong to his firstborn son "went to the place he was thinking of"—that is, to Rachel, who would eventually become the mother of Joseph. On the other hand, Jacob had been innocent in his intentions. Therefore Reuven, his firstborn with Leah, was not anathematized.

For Kabbalah, sexuality is the ultimate proving ground of the principle that consciousness creates reality. The reality in question is nothing other than the child that is born out of a particular union. Science teaches that the characteristics of that child derive from a complex interplay of genetic factors, but Kabbalah emphasizes not only the spiritual status of the lovers, but even the thoughts that are passing through their minds. At every moment, the Zohar calls on us to recognize our mission in the world and conduct ourselves accordingly. In its interpretation of stories like Jacob and Rachel's, it also shows how difficult that is to accomplish.

CHAPTER 18

JACOB'S TRIALS

Vol. 6, pp. 4–20

"And Jacob dwelt in the land in which his father so-journed, in the land of Cna'an." (Genesis 31:1) Rabbi Chiya opened the discussion with the verse: "Many are the afflictions of the righteous, and Hashem delivers him out of them all." (Psalms 34:21) Come and behold: how many enemies a person must face from the day that the Creator gives him a soul in this world! As soon as we come into the world, the evil inclination is immediately ready to join us, as it is written: "Sin crouches at the door." (Genesis 4:7)

The human body is a pure manifestation of the desire to receive for the self alone. Because of this, our soul confronts the negative inclination at the moment it enters a physical self. But we should make a distinction between this kabbalistic principle of the body under the sway of the "evil inclination" and other, moralistic religious teachings that the body itself is evil or unclean. Kabbalistically, the body is simply a "target of opportunity" for the Adversary, as are all occasions of potential growth and transformation.

Each of us arrives here on the physical plane with our own particular evil inclination, our own sin crouching at the door. But neither the evil inclination nor the negative actions that flow from it should be construed as malign. The English word *sin* derives from the Latin *sine,* meaning "without." Kabbalistically, our sin is what we are without, that is, our sin is our lack, the particular spot—or spots—where we are without Light. When we come to *Malchut* it is in order that we may correct our lack, allow it to become Light-filled.

The evil inclination cannot attach itself to us indiscriminately. It must look for an opening. We must "invite it in." The evil inclination is like a nocturnal insect. It is drawn to the Light, but it cannot enter a dwelling unless a window has been left open.

Our lack is specific to each of us in accord with our needed spiritual correction. It may manifest as a physical handicap, mental or emotional distress, perilous living conditions, lack of love or family, or poverty, to name merely a handful of the infinite array of possible deficits we may experience in our human life. This is not to suggest that there is a direct corollary between any possible affliction we experience and what we perceive as our incompleteness. These are simply the challenges we have been given this time around which, when overcome with grace, allow us to transform and make ourselves whole.

So what is it then that accounts for the *particular expression* of lack that each of us knows as his or her own?

To answer that, let us contemplate Exodus 20:4, in which God forbids the worship of pagan gods. He says, "Thou shalt not bow down unto them nor serve them. For I, the Lord thy God, am a jealous God, visiting the iniquities [sins] of the fathers upon the children unto the third and fourth generation of them that hate me." This verse frequently comes under criticism because it is most often interpreted to mean that God, seemingly unjust, punishes succeeding generations of the innocent for the misdeeds of an individual man or woman. Today, one can make a strong case for this interpretation when we think of the short-term greed that has produced chemical and radiation pollution of air and water with little or no thought given to future side effects. We see all too clearly the result of this sin in babies born with birth defects and congenital illnesses. Be that as it may, Kabbalah offers a very different view of this passage.

"Sins of the fathers" does not mean what it appears to on the surface. What it really indicates is that a given individual, sent into this world for the purpose of correction, fails to complete that correction and must return. The biblical verse is not meant to imply that the child must pay for his or her father's or grandfather's negative acts, but rather that the individual who has committed the sin literally is the father, *returned* in the third or fourth generation to pick up the task of correction where he left it. He is merely reaping what he has sown in an earlier lifetime; he has become his own great- or great-great-grandchild.

Kabbalist Isaac Luria (the Ari) said that the number of times the cycle must be repeated before correction is achieved depends on the individual soul. However, if that soul lives one lifetime with no progress, it is allowed to return only three more times to attempt that particular correction. In the literal translation of Exodus the word *generation* is not mentioned. If we know that, the meaning then is clear: A man or woman may return three more times for a total of four lives. If progress is made in any of those incarnations, then no further limit is imposed on the number of reincarnations needed to complete the mission of correction. But even while making correction in one area, we must still beware of the negative force that crouches in wait to see if, perhaps, another door may open to its chaos and degradation.

While some of our afflictions assume manifest forms, in their negativity they are nonetheless "lacks." Others are easier to see in this light because we recognize them as absences rather than presences. But many are not perceived as afflictions at all. Certainly Job endured the first two categories: His body was covered with boils, and his wealth and his family were taken away. But he was also afflicted before any of these things befell him, by complacency in an environment that was too indulgent for spiritual growth to take hold. Jacob's afflictions were somewhat different from Job's, but no less punishing.

The Zohar gives us the description.

> Come and behold, it is written: "And Jacob dwelt in the land in which his father sojourned." (Genesis 37:1) What is meant by "his father sojourned"? It means terror from every side, because Isaac was anxious and afraid all his days. Rabbi Elazar said: "And Jacob dwelt" in this place that was in darkness. "The land in which his father sojourned" refers to precisely this fear.

The Zohar always interprets physical space in emotional and spiritual terms. When the text says that Jacob "dwelt in the land where his father sojourned," this means that he experienced the same pain that had tormented Isaac. The playing out of inner conflict over generations is a persistent but elusive theme in the biblical narrative. The Creator, it seems, uses genealogy both to hide and reveal His mercy and His judgment.

It is said that Esau transmitted his hatred of Jacob throughout the generations, beginning with his descendant Haman, whose attempt to exterminate the people of Israel is chronicled in the biblical book of Esther. But it is also true that even Jacob's descendants must atone for his actions, however benign they might seem.

Thus, Jacob and his progeny were held accountable, not for stealing Esau's blessing, but for causing Esau to cry out in pain.

The Zohar explains that we create sufferings for ourselves, and for our descendants who are extensions of ourselves:

> Come and behold: this is true. From the day of birth, beasts protect themselves by fleeing from fire and evil places. Yet man immediately flings himself into the fire, because the evil inclination dwells within him and prompts him to follow the path of evil.

Do we really fling ourselves into the fire? Unfortunately, yes—but often without realizing what we are doing. So much energy is wasted by humankind in the pursuit of things that are ultimately meaningless, while we avoid experiences that can foster spiritual growth. Often when we are drawn to the flames, it is because we do not know we will be burned. We may not even recognize the fire! It may be disguised as a very profitable business deal, an exciting relationship, or a chance to escape some unpleasant responsibility. But "escaping responsibility" is actually "escaping" our spiritual growth. We are not transformed by keeping within our comfort zones. Transformation requires real effort.

> For we have learned: "Better is a poor and wise child than an old and foolish king who knows not how to take care of himself." (Ecclesiastes 14:13) Better is a child, because a child represents the good inclination; a child has been in the world for only a short time.

The Zohar's concern and admiration for children is one of its most remarkable qualities. In ancient and medieval literature, children are rarely given much attention except as expressions of their parents' wealth or fecundity. But as we discussed in chapter 8 ("The Unnameable"), Kabbalah teaches that children are sacred beings who have just recently been with God. There may be aspects of the Zohar that seem out of synch with our time, but its pronounced affection for children and its awareness of our responsibilities to them is strikingly contemporary.

> In the verse: ". . . than an old and foolish king" (Ecclesiastes 4:13), the word "king" refers to the evil inclination, which is called a "king" and "ruler of people in the world." It is certainly "old," and "foolish," because as soon as man is born and comes into the world, it lives with him.
>
> Further it reads: ". . . who knows not how to take care of himself." It is not written: "to take care of others," but, "to take care of himself." Why? Because the king is foolish, and Solomon said: "The fool walks in darkness" (Ecclesiastes 2:14), because the fool comes from darkness and will never have light.

Evil is foolish in the sense that it ignores the obvious. The Creator desires only to bestow His gifts upon us, yet the evil inclination turns us away. A person who follows this inclination does not understand how to take care of himself—that is, of his soul—in the most basic sense. "The fool comes from darkness" means that his thoughts and feelings originate in negativity, and therefore he cannot live in a way that brings transformation and fulfillment.

> Come and behold: This is why the evil inclination comes to join with man as soon as possible, from the

day he is born, so that man will believe in it. Later, when the good inclination arrives, man will find it difficult to believe, and its words will seem burdensome. Similarly, we have learned that he who is a subtle evil-monger hastens to plead his case in front of a judge before the arrival of his colleague, the litigant, as written: "The one who pleads first seems to be in the right." (Proverbs 18:17)

"The serpent was craftier." (Genesis 3:2) He, too, hurries to dwell in man before his colleague, the good inclination, comes to dwell in him. And because he arrived early to plead his case, when, his colleague, who is the good inclination, comes later, it is difficult for man to unite with it! And he cannot raise his head, as if he carried on his shoulders the burdens of the world. All this is because the Evil One came first. Of this, Solomon said, "The poor man's wisdom is despised and his words are not heard" (Ecclesiastes 9:16), because the other arrived earlier. For any judge who accepts the words of a litigant before his colleague arrives, it is as if he accepts another deity to believe in. A righteous person suffers many afflictions in this world in order not to believe in and join the evil inclination. And the Creator saves him from all. As it is written: "Many are the afflictions of the righteous, and God delivers him out of them all." (Psalms 34:20)

We are all on our way to becoming righteous and while we cannot avoid our trials, in every instance that we make proactive progress toward the goal of spiritual correction the Creator assists and protects us.

Come and behold: how many afflictions befell Jacob to keep him from becoming infected by the evil inclination, and to keep evil distant from his lot. He suffered punishments and afflictions, and had no quiet repose. He said: "I had no repose, nor had I rest, nor was I quiet; yet trouble came." (Job 3:26) How many afflictions did Jacob have to suffer! As it is written: "I had no repose" in Laban's house, and I could not escape from him. "Nor had I rest" because of that suffering that Esau's minister inflicted on me. And after that, there was the fear of Esau himself. "Nor was I quiet," on account of Dinah and Shechem. Come and behold: how many afflictions do the righteous suffer in this world? Trouble after trouble, pain after pain, so that they can merit the world to come.

"And Jacob dwelt in the land in which his father had sojourned, in the land of Cna'an." Rabbi Yosi opened the discussion with the verse: "The righteous perish, and no man lays it to heart: and merciful men are taken away, none considering that the righteous is taken away from the evil to come." (Isaiah 57:1) "The righteous perish" when the Creator looks on the world and it is not as it should be, and Judgment falls. Then the righteous are taken away so that the Judgment will fall only on the others, who will have no protection.

It may seem to us that the "taking away of the righteous," presumably by death, is a more stern decree than whatever befalls the wicked, who at least remain alive. In these passages, however, the Zohar is not speaking of the death of the young and the innocent as an aspect of the everyday world. That phenomenon is addressed elsewhere (chapter 24, "Why the Wicked Are So Strong"), but here the reference is to the Final Judgment, in which the righteous are removed from the scene for the same reason Noah entered the ark: to make way for the final cleansing of the world.

> As long as the righteous dwell in this world, Final Judgment cannot be handed down on it. What is the origin of this principle? From Moshe, as it is written: "He said that He would destroy them, had not Moshe His chosen one stood before Him in the breach." (Psalms 106:23) Thus, the Holy One, blessed be He, takes the righteous from among them and elevates them from this world. Only then does He deliver His due retribution to the others, as the last part of the passage reads: "The righteous are taken away from the evil to come." In the days of Joseph, exile was avoided because Joseph protected the people of Israel throughout his life. But when he died, exile immediately befell them, as it is written: "And Joseph died . . ." (Exodus 1:6) which is followed by, "Come, let us deal wisely with them" (Ibid. 10), and "they made their lives bitter." (Ibid. 14) Similarly, wherever a righteous person dwells in the world, the Creator protects the world for his sake.

A kabbalistic tale suggests a path that we might follow if we are to avoid having the sins of the father visited upon the future expressions of our soul in the physical world. The story is of a man who dreamed that he had been called before the judgment of heaven. A wagon arrived filled with white rocks, which angels placed on a large scale. "These represent the good deeds you've done in your life," one of the angels told the dreamer.

When the rocks had been weighed, another wagon arrived, this one filled with black rocks representing all the negative actions the man had done. As these rocks were weighed, and the scale disclosed the awful truth: the bad deeds outweighed the good. Now the man was terrified. Would he be condemned for all eternity?

Just then, much to his surprise, a third wagon arrived filled with rocks and stones of many different colors. The man was puzzled. "What are these?" he asked.

"These represent the challenges you accepted during your lifetime," an angel said, placing the colored rocks along with the white ones from the first wagon. "Each rock is an obstacle you faced, or a difficulty you accepted and overcame." To the man's great joy and relief, the addition of the many-colored rocks tipped the scale in his favor.

When his eyes opened after this dream, the man was also truly awakened in a spiritual sense. All the things he had tried to avoid in his life—all the aches and pains he had complained about, the bills he had to pay, the people whom he found so annoying—were suddenly seen in a very different light. He had always sought ways to make his life easier. Now he could hardly wait to start seeking challenges for the sake of his soul.

The Zohar tells us that spiritual development is difficult and is meant to be difficult. Yet the world we live in today is filled with "labor-saving" devices. In almost every area of life, we have come to believe that to the extent something is easy, it is to be preferred over something that is hard. But this value system has severe limitations in some of the most important areas of life. Learning to walk, for example, is not easy, nor is learning to speak or to read. Yet these are activities that we are meant to do. They are hardwired into our neurophysiology. A child does not give up trying to walk regardless of how many falls take place. In fact, the falls themselves have many benefits, and this is also true in spirituality. Kabbalah should never be portrayed as a "feel-good" philosophy. From the struggle of

Abraham and Sarah to have a child, through Jacob's experiences in Canaan and the people of Israel's bondage in Egypt, the patriarchs and matriarchs confront seemingly hopeless difficulties—and they face those trials not just with hope, but with certainty. In all of Kabbalah, no lesson is more important than this one.

JOSEPH IN THE PIT

Jacob loved Joseph best of all his twelve sons, and there were two reasons for this. First, he foresaw the greatness that would come to Joseph—not in detail, but simply with an intuition for the leadership role that would fall to him. Second, he loved Joseph for his devotion to Torah study and for the knowledge that he had already amassed even as a boy. Jacob was certainly not wrong in his assessments of Joseph, but he treated Joseph differently than his other children. The famous "coat of many colors" that Joseph received from Jacob is an expression of this. The coat formalized Jacob's sense that Joseph was of high spiritual rank. It was a sacred object, made from Rachel's bridal gown, but its design also had practical implications. The midrash describes the coat as having long sleeves, making it unsuitable for manual labor, with the implication that the wearer was exempt from hard physical work.

This issue of Jacob's favoritism is explicitly raised in the Talmud. The Zohar is consistently reluctant to criticize the conduct of a patriarch in the way we might speak of an ordinary individual. Doing so compares the biblical characters to our own era of less elevated thoughts and motives. Still, within the environment of Joseph's family, the biblical narrative suggests that people might have conducted themselves with more discretion. This includes not only Jacob but also Joseph himself.

In his youth, the Bible depicts Joseph as an almost angelic person who, in the artless way of someone who is perfectly good, was unaware of the effect he had on people of less elevated spiritual status. When Joseph observed his brothers apparently committing a violation of the dietary laws, he simply told Jacob about it—which the brothers understandably failed to appreciate. Joseph also spoke to his brothers about his dreams, which foretold his destiny as a leader over them. Therefore, as the Bible expresses it (Genesis 37:4), "his brothers hated him." So when, at Isaac's behest, Joseph traveled to join his brothers in the land of Dothan, where they were pasturing sheep, the brothers thought of killing him and hiding his body in a pit. "Behold, the dreamer is coming," they said to each other. "We shall see what will become of his dreams." But when Reuven, the eldest among them, prevailed upon them to spare his life, the brothers threw him into a pit alive. Secretly, Reuven planned to come and release Joseph after the others were gone.

Joseph, gentle by nature, was terrified at being imprisoned in a hole in the ground. He sought to turn his thoughts to the Torah, but his fear made his mind a blank. With Joseph's captivity as a starting point, the Zohar first celebrates the presence of Torah in the lives of the righteous and then describes hell as the withdrawal of that presence.

Vol. 6, pp. 64–66

"And they took him, and cast him into a pit: and that pit was empty; there was no water in it." (Genesis 37:24) Rabbi Yehuda opened the discussion with the verse: "The Torah of Hashem is perfect, restoring the soul." (Psalms 19:8) Men should endeavor to study the Torah as much as possible, for whoever does so gains life in this world and in the world to come, and he merits both worlds. Even he who strives to study the Torah, but does it for worldly reasons, merits reward in this world and escapes Judgment in the next.

Come and behold, it is written: "Length of days is in her right hand; and in her left hand are riches and honor." (Proverbs 3:16) "Length of days," refers to that person who endeavors to study the Torah for its own sake, for he has the everlasting world. "And in her left hand are riches and honor," refers to reward and peace in this world.

Whoever studies the Torah for its own sake will find that when he passes from the world, the Torah goes before him with proclamations and protects him from approaching accusers. It guards his body in the grave, and when his soul departs to ascend to its place, it precedes the soul. Many gates are thrown open before the Torah until it brings the soul to its place. And when the dead are resurrected, the Torah speaks in that man's favor.

"When you walk, it shall lead you; when you lie down, it shall keep you and when you awake, it shall talk with you." (Proverbs 6:22) "When you walk, it shall lead you," refers to the Torah that goes before a man when he dies. "When you lie down, it shall keep you," refers to the interval when the body lies in the grave, for at that time the body is judged and sentenced and the Torah acts in its defense. "And when you awake, it shall talk with you," refers to the time at which the dead rise from the dust.

Rabbi Elazar quoted the verse: "It shall talk with you." (Proverbs 6:22) Although the dead have just risen from the dust, they remember the Torah they studied before their death. They will know all they studied before departing the world. And everything shall be clearer than it was before death, for whatever he strove to understand yet did not successfully grasp, is now clear in his innermost parts. And the Torah speaks within him. This is the meaning of the verse: "And when you awake, it shall talk with you." (Proverbs 6:22) Rabbi Yehuda said that whoever studied the Torah diligently in this world deserves to be occupied with it in the world to come.

Come and behold: a man who did not have the merit to be occupied with the Torah in this world walks in darkness. When he passes from the world, he is put in the lowest place in Gehenom, where no one pities him, a place described as a "gruesome pit," a "miry clay," as it is written: "He brought me up also out of the gruesome pit, out of the miry clay, and set my feet upon a rock, and established my footsteps." (Psalms 40:3)

Reuven should have protected Joseph more diligently. He did not explicitly sin, but, like Aaron at the time of the golden calf, he tried to finesse a solution to a difficult situation in which he was outnumbered. Kabbalah esteems those who take a clear and ardent stand under those circumstances, even if the antagonist is the Creator himself, as was the case with Moses (Exodus 32:31–32).

"And they took him, and cast him into a pit." (Genesis 37:24) They cast Joseph into the pit, where the secret of the faith does not abide. Water is the secret of the faith, and when it is written, "And the pit was empty," this refers to the secret of the faith. But Rabbi Yitzchak said: There were snakes and scorpions in the pit. Why then is it written of Reuven, "He might save him out of their hands"? Did not Reuven fear that the snakes and scorpions would harm Joseph? If so, how did he plan "to deliver him back to his father . . . that he might save him"? Reuven thought it was better to cast him into the pit of snakes and scorpions than to deliver him to his enemies, who have no compassion for him. Thus, the saying: "Rather should a man throw himself into a fire or a pit full of serpents and scorpions, than be delivered into the hands of his enemies." For if a man is righteous here in a place of snakes and scorpions, the Creator performs miracles for him, or sometimes he is saved by the merit of his fathers. But once delivered into the hands of enemies, few escape.

Come and behold: As punishment for neglecting the study of the Torah, Israel was exiled from the Holy Land—only for being removed from and leaving the Torah. This is explained by the verse, "Who is the wise man, that may understand this? Why does the land perish . . . ? Because they have forsaken My Torah which I set before them." (Jeremiah 9:11–12) Rabbi Yosi said: "Therefore My people are gone into captivity, because they have no knowledge." (Isaiah 5:13) Hence, everything is based on the existence of the Torah, and the world only endures by means of the Torah, which sustains the worlds above and below. As it is written: "If my Covenant be not day and night, it were as if

I had not appointed the ordinances of heaven and earth . . ." (Jeremiah 33:25)

In reading the story of Joseph and his brothers, our tendency may be to get caught up in the family drama. The Creator views things in a much broader context. It had been ordained that the people of Israel would undergo exile in Egypt. Whatever the ethics of their behavior toward him, the brothers' violence against Joseph furthered God's intentions. When the brothers sold Joseph as a slave to traders on their way to Egypt, the foundation was laid not only for the exile, but also for the eventual escape and the revelation at Mount Sinai.

In Kabbalah, the wiser person is always the one who sees the bigger picture. From that perspective, Joseph's brothers were performing a positive service in implementing God's will, though they seem culpable within a narrower view of the story. Kabbalah makes it very clear, however, that they were highly evolved souls— *tzaddikim,* in fact. They believed that Joseph had harbored evil intentions against them with the criticisms he brought to Isaac. Moreover, as with all the important biblical characters, they experienced life as individual human beings, but also as builders of the spiritual architecture and instruments of the Creator's will. It was His will that the people should experience exile in Egypt. Of necessity, that meant that Joseph must be thrown into the pit. From Kabbalah's viewpoint, those who carried out this act were serving a purpose that cannot be understood in terms of situational ethics.

The fact is that it is not always possible to perceive why certain things happen. Our challenge is to trust in the big picture—to know, though we cannot see it, that the oak is in the acorn.

CHAPTER 20

JOSEPH IN EGYPT

Joseph's ability to see his own future in dreams, and to interpret the dreams of others, is the foundation of his success in the world. Exactly how this came about is carefully narrated by the Zohar.

In the passages that follow Egypt is really an extension of the pit into which Joseph was thrown by his brothers. Thus, he is described as "brought down" into Egypt, where he becomes the property of Potiphar, whom most biblical commentators identify as Pharaoh's executioner. Egypt is a land of negative energy and self-serving magic. We are in Egypt, according to Kabbalah, whenever we are in bondage spiritually. Yet as we saw in the previous chapter, the sojourn of Joseph and the people of Israel was divinely ordained. Just as Joseph had to be placed in the pit, the people collectively had to be laid low in order to rise again.

Vol. 6, pp. 101–139

In the verse, "And Joseph was brought down to Egypt; and Potiphar bought him" (Genesis 39:1), why is it written: "brought down" rather than "went down"? The Creator consented to the act of selling Joseph to

Egypt, so that His decree would be fulfilled, as it is written: "Know surely that your seed shall be a stranger." (Genesis 15:13) And Potiphar bought him, to commit the sin of sodomy with him.

". . . who commands the sun, and it rises not . . ." (Job 9:7) Rabbi Shimon says this refers to Joseph when he was sold into Egypt. And of his brothers it is written: "And the eleven stars bowed down to me." (Genesis 37:9) In another explanation, "Who commands the sun," refers to Jacob at the time he was told: "know now whether it be your son's coat or not." (Genesis 37:32)

The sun darkened and the stars did not shine because Joseph was separated from his father. Since Joseph was sold, Jacob abstained from marital intercourse and remained in mourning until he heard the good tidings of Joseph.

That is, many years would pass before the aged Jacob received word that his favorite son was alive and well.

Come and behold: Wherever the Righteous go, the Holy One, blessed be He, protects them and never abandons them. As David said, "Even though I walk through the valley of the shadow of death, I will fear no evil: for You are with me." (Psalms 23:4) For wherever the righteous go, the Shechinah never leaves them.

When Joseph walked the valley of the shadow of death and was brought down to Egypt, the Shechinah was with him, as it is written: "And the Creator was with Joseph." (Genesis 39:2) Because the Shechinah was with him, whatever he did prospered. If he had something in his hand, but his master asked for something else, what was in his hand would turn into that which his master wanted, as it is written: "And his master saw that Hashem was with him, and that Hashem made all that he did prosper in his hand." (Genesis 39:3) Assuredly, it "did prosper in his hand," for Hashem was with him.

Potiphar was amazed by the capabilities of his handsome young slave. No matter what he asked for, it instantly appeared in Joseph's hand. As a true Egyptian, Potiphar at first ascribed this to sorcery. But it was really the Light of the Creator, to which Joseph's soul remained unfailingly connected. Even Potiphar eventually saw that Joseph's powers derived from something beyond his understanding. As it is written, "And his master saw that the Creator was with him, and that the Creator made all that he did to prosper in his hand." (Genesis 39:3)

Come and behold, it is not written: "And his master knew that Hashem was with him," but rather "And his master *saw*." He saw with his own eyes the miracles that the Holy One, blessed be He, performed by His hand. Therefore, "Hashem blessed the Egyptian house for Joseph's sake." (Genesis 39:5) The Holy One, blessed be He, preserves the righteous. For the sake of the righteous, He also protects the wicked. This is said in the verse: "Hashem has blessed the house of Oved Edom . . . because of the ark of Elohim." (II Samuel 6:12)

But while Potiphar and his household were blessed through Joseph's presence, Joseph himself was soon to be severely tried.

Other people are blessed for the sake of the righteous, but the righteous themselves cannot be saved by their own merits. Joseph's master has been blessed for his sake, yet Joseph could not be saved by his merits and gain his freedom.

Because of his faithful service, Potiphar put Joseph in charge of his entire estate. But then Potiphar's wife became attracted to Joseph and tried to seduce him. When Joseph rejected her, she accused him of trying to commit rape, and based on her accusations, Joseph was thrown into prison.

This is a complex story that has many interpretations. But as a first step to understanding it, the sages look backward in the biblical narrative to an incident that almost seems to have been misplaced. Comprising the 38th chapter of Genesis, it is inserted between Joseph's being sold into slavery and his arrival in Potiphar's household. It concerns Judah, the son of Leah, who married a Canaanite woman named Shua, who then gave birth to Er, Onan, and Shela. Er, the eldest son, married Tamar, but Er was evil and the Creator removed him from the world. Onan, according to the law, was obligated to marry Tamar, his childless brother's wife. But he was also evil and was taken away. Now Tamar was to marry the youngest and only surviving son, Shela. But Shela was too young, and, based on what had already happened, Judah was worried that Shela might also die before his time. So Judah asked Tamar to return to her father's house until Shela grew up. The Bible then relates that Judah's wife died. When he visited the town in which Tamar resided, she disguised herself as a prostitute and had relations with Judah.

Here the Torah returns to the story of Joseph. But why is Joseph's story interrupted by that of Tamar? The kabbalists explain that both stories are about women whose initial intentions were good. They recognized men of high spiritual status, and they wanted to bear the children of these men. Tamar's thoughts, according to the commentaries, were pure and for the sake of heaven. So were those of Potiphar's wife, who had been told by fortune tellers that Joseph's offspring would issue from her. What she did not realize, however, was that her daughter would later marry Joseph and have children with him, and not she herself. Frustrated and confused, her worthy feelings for Joseph turned first into lust and then into vindictive anger.

Still, her first thought had been to bring forth children from Joseph the Righteous. But here Kabbalah teaches that, in spiritual matters, making a good beginning is not enough. The distance between the beginning and end is often very great, and always greater than we expect. True spiritual work requires maintaining our strength in order to manifest good in the end.

The Zohar tells the story of Potiphar's wife with a decidedly negative slant.

> He was put in prison, as it is written: "Whose foot they hurt with fetters he was laid in iron." (Psalms 105: 18) Subsequently, the Holy One, blessed be He, set him free and made him ruler over Egypt. As it is written: "For Hashem loves justice and forsakes not His pious ones; they are preserved forever." (Psalms 37:28) He protects the righteous in this world and in the world to come, as it is written: "But let all those that put their trust in You rejoice: let them ever shout for joy, because You do defend them; and let those who love Your name be joyful in You." (Psalms 5:12)
>
> Rabbi Elazar asks: What is the meaning of the verse, "And it came to pass after these things"? (Gene-

sis 39:7) Joseph gave the evil inclination an opening for accusations, when it was said that Joseph's father was mourning over him and that he, Joseph, adorned himself and curled his hair. This aroused against him the bear—that is, Potiphar's wife—and it assailed him.

It is written: "And it came to pass, as she spoke to Joseph day by day." (Genesis 39:10) "As she spoke," refers to the evil side, who daily ascends to bring accusations before the Holy One, blessed be He, as well as evil reports and slander, in order to destroy men.

It is written: "that he hearkened not to her, to lie by her, or to be with her" (Genesis 39:10) because the Creator is compassionate towards the world; "to lie by her" means to allow her to rule over the world, for she cannot govern without permission. Were it not for the help obtained from above, not one man would remain in the world. But the Holy One, blessed be He, pities the world.

Rabbi Yitzchak said that in the future, the righteous will see the evil inclination as a high mountain and wonder how we could have conquered such a high and huge mountain. The wicked will see the evil inclination as a thread that is as thin as a hair. They will marvel and ask: How could we not have overcome such a tiny thread of hair? These weep, and the others weep. The Holy One, blessed be He, will sweep the wicked from the world and slay him before their eyes, so he will not have dominion over the world anymore. The Righteous will see it and rejoice, as it is written: "Surely the righteous shall give thanks to your name: the upright shall dwell in your presence." (Psalms 140:124)

It was in prison that the greatest opportunity of Joseph's life unexpectedly presented itself. Just as the Light attracts the negative powers, darkness can also attract Light. It is said that "nature abhors a vacuum," and this is as true in spiritual matters as it is in the physical world.

Genesis 40

It came to pass that the butler of the King of Egypt and his baker had offended their lord . . . and he put them into the prison, into the place where Joseph was bound. . . . And they dreamed a dream both of them, each man his dream in one night.

The Zohar comments:

> Come and behold: The Holy One, blessed be He, transforms matters in the world so as to lift the heads of the righteous. To enable Joseph to raise his head for being righteous before Him, He caused the master to be angry with his servants, as it is written: "The butler of the king of Egypt, and his baker, offended their lord the king of Egypt." (Genesis 40:1) All this happened to lift the head of Joseph the Righteous. He was humiliated by his brothers through a dream, and he obtained greatness over his brothers and was raised above the whole world through a dream.

The butler had dreamed of a vine blossoming with three branches of grapes, and from this Joseph inferred that the butler would be freed from prison three days later. Encouraged by this, the baker revealed his own dream: He was walking with three baskets stacked on his head, and birds came to eat from the baskets. Much to the baker's distress, Joseph's interpretation predicted that he would be condemned to die within three days.

In the Zohar's own interpretation, the dreams refer to the destiny of the people of Israel:

> "Let a double portion of your spirit be upon me" (Genesis 40:9), Joseph trembled because he did not know what it meant. But when he added, "And on the vine were three tendrils" (Genesis 40:10), his spirit rose. Joseph said: "This is assuredly an altogether good tiding," for the vine indicated the Congregation of Israel.
>
> ". . . and it was as though it budded, and its blossoms shot forth." (Genesis 40:10) For their sake, the congregation of Israel arises and is blessed by the Supernal King, ". . . and its clusters brought forth ripe grapes," refers to the righteous of the world, who are likened to ripened grapes. Another explanation of the verse, "and its clusters brought forth ripe grapes," is that it refers to the wine preserved in its grapes since the six days of Creation.

Recall that the fruit of the Tree of Knowledge was not an apple but a cluster of grapes.

> Come and behold: Adam's wife pressed him grapes and brought death upon him, Israel, and the whole world. When Noah came upon these grapes, he was not well guarded, as it is written: "He drank of the wine, and was drunk; and he was uncovered within his tent." (Genesis 9:21) The sons of Aaron drank wine and offered a sacrifice while still under its influence. It is

therefore written: "Their grapes are grapes of gall, their clusters are bitter." (Deuteronomy 32:32)

The chief butler saw in his dream good grapes in the vineyard, where they sent forth pleasantness and fragrance. Joseph looked into the root of the matter and solved it thoroughly. Because he received good tidings by that dream, he interpreted it favorably, and so it came to pass.

Come and behold, it is written: "When the chief baker saw that the interpretation was good, he said to Joseph, 'I also in my dream had three baskets of white bread on my head.'" (Genesis 40:16) Damned are the wicked, whose every deed is for evil, whose every speech is uttered for evil and to cause evil.

The baker began his speech with the word "*af*" (which means "also," but can also mean "anger") in the sentence, "I also in my dream . . ." Immediately, Joseph was seized with fright, for he knew that all his words were of evil intent and that he bore evil tidings. By the verse: "Behold, I had three baskets of white bread on my head," Joseph knew that he was a part of the destruction of the Temple and the exile of Israel from the Holy Land.

Come and behold: "And in the uppermost basket there was all manner of Pharaoh's baked food; and the birds did eat them out of the basket upon my head." (Genesis 40:17) This refers to the other nations, who will gather upon Israel to kill them, destroy their homes, and scatter them to the four winds of the world. Joseph saw all this and knew that this dream alluded to Israel, who would be guilty before the King.

He then interpreted his dream in an evil sense, which
was fulfilled.

Kabbalah teaches that dream interpretation is a delicate matter,
and only the very knowledgeable will be able to understand the true
messages that are concealed inside a dream. Yet it is critically important that our dreams receive interpretation. As the Talmud puts
it, "A dream that is not understood is like a letter that remains un-
opened."

If a positive dream is ignored, it remains mere potential. With
time the content of the dream becomes stagnant, and it is much
more difficult for the positive elements of the dream to manifest in
our life. With apparently negative dreams the need for interpretation is even greater. If we do not understand the messages of such
dreams, we can miss the specific point of correction that may very
well be what we came into this world to achieve. When negative
circumstances remain unresolved in the external world, and if our
inner character also remains unchanged, an opening is created for
chaos and negativity to manifest. "Ignorance of the law is no ex-
cuse," and failure to pay attention to our dreams is a quite willful
form of ignorance.

But even as it enjoins us to interpret our dreams, Kabbalah cautions us regarding the choice of an interpreter because, according to
Kabbalah, the way a dream is interpreted is the way it will come
to pass in the material world. It is said that at the time of the second temple there were twenty-four interpreters of dreams in
Jerusalem. If a person told his dream to all twenty-four interpreters,
the dreamer might very well receive twenty-four different interpretations. Yet each of the interpretations would have the potential
to actually play itself out in the world. Because the very act of interpretation can be a self-confirming prophecy, the Zohar teaches

that interpretation of a dream is more important than the dream itself. We should make every effort to find the right person to interpret our dreams—someone who truly loves and cares for us individually, or a deeply spiritual person who cares for all humankind.

When we reveal our dreams to those who wish us well, we create an opportunity for them to express their good wishes and for the universe to affirm their positive interpretation. Most important, we should never ignore or forget our dreams, for a dream that is gone from the mind can never be realized in the material world. Joseph kept his dreams in the forefront of his consciousness and was always expecting their fulfillment.

CHAPTER 21

THE GOLDEN CALF

A s the subject of historical paintings and poetry, as well as a show-stopping scene in Cecil B. DeMille's biblical epic film *The Ten Commandments*, the incident of the golden calf is usually depicted as a lurid set piece of idol worship and orgy. But the Zohar interprets it as a complex drama involving spiritual forces that came into play even before the sin of Adam—and the greatest missed opportunity in human history.

Exodus 32:1–6

When the people saw that Moses was so long in coming down from the mountain, the people gathered against Aaron and said to him, "Come, make us a god who shall go before us, for that man Moses, who brought us from the land of Egypt—we do not know what has happened to him." Aaron said to them, "Take off the gold rings that are on the ears of your wives, your sons, and your daughters, and bring them to me." And all the people took off the gold rings that were in their ears and brought them to Aaron. Then he took them and wrapped them in linen, and made a molten calf. And they exclaimed, "This is your god, O Israel, who brought you out of the land of Egypt!" When Aaron saw this, he built an altar before the calf; and Aaron announced: "Tomorrow shall be a festival of the Lord!" Early next day, the people offered up burnt offerings and brought sacrifices of well-being; they sat down to eat and drink, and then rose to dance.

While the Torah's narrative of these incidents is typically brief, the Zohar uses it as the starting point for a careful examination of what happened before, during, and after.

Vol. 12, pp. 133–158

"And the people saw that Moses delayed." Who are "the people"? The Torah calls them the mixed multitude. But were they Ludim and Cushim and Caftorim and Tugarmim? No, they were Egyptians, and they had traveled with Israel out of Egypt. Had they been a mixture of many nations, the Torah would have said so. But the Torah does not mention the names of nations, because they were all of one nation.

At the time that Moses performed miracles in Egypt, all the magicians and sorcerers of Egypt had been there. They wanted to compete with the miracles of the Creator, as it is written, "The sorcerers of Egypt did the same with their spells." But when they saw the wonders that Moses performed, they came to him asking to be converted. The Creator said to Moses, "Do not accept them." Moses said, "Master of the world, let them see your mighty deeds every day and they will know that there is no Elohim except you." And Moses accepted them.

Is it surprising that Moses not only argues with God but also disobeys the Creator's directive? Kabbalah teaches that we are partners with God in the ongoing construction of the many dimensions of reality. We are not puppets. This partnership role was especially apparent to the biblical patriarchs and matriarchs, who were aware that they were building the foundations of the spiritual edifice. With this sense of responsibility, Moses was willing to question God, and even go against his advice.

The magicians of Egypt were in the mixed multitude, and at their head were Junus and Jambrus. These people gathered themselves before Aaron. Until now the mixed multitude had been subdued, but now they arose and said to him, "Include us among Israel with you, as one nation. Otherwise, make a god who shall go before us. Let a god go before us, as your god goes before you."

Aaron thought, "The holy nation should not mingle with these people as one." So he said to them, "Break off the golden rings that are on the ears of your wives, your sons, and your daughters, and bring them to me." He thought that their wives and their children would resist giving up their gold, and perhaps while they were quarreling Moses would return. But as it is written, "All the people broke off the golden rings that were in their ears." And in their hearts many of people of Israel also joined with the mixed multitude.

Aaron did not protect himself from Junus and Jambrus, the two magicians who were at the head of the mixed multitude. These two divided the gold between them, one taking two thirds and the other taking one third. Through the sixth hour of the day they did their sorcery and their enchantments. As the seventh hour arrived, they both took gold in their hands, and they raised their hands to the hands of Aaron. As it is written, "And he took from their hand." As soon as he received the gold from their hands a voice came out and said, "They who join hands for wicked ends shall not go unpunished." Because they have brought evil into the world.

If Aaron would have said to them, "First put the gold onto the ground, and I will take from the ground," then they would not have been able to accomplish anything with their sorcery. But he took it from their hands. See what Aaron did, the prophet, the wise man. He did not know how to guard himself. For had he taken the gold from the ground, then all the magicians in the world would not have been successful.

Evil after evil. First, the evil that he accepted it from their hand. Second, the evil that he did not throw it on the ground. And third, the evil that he wrapped it in linen and concealed it from the eye. He placed all the gold into one bag, and it was guarded from sight. Then everything became manifest.

The magicians say it must be thus with this kind of magic, because things that will be revealed must first be concealed and covered. First it must be concealed from the eye, and then the magician goes into his craft to reveal it.

But Heaven forbid that Aaron made the calf, for it is written in the Torah, "He took the calf that they made." And it is not written, "that he made it." When it is written, "He took from their hand," and when it is also written, "He fashioned it," this means that by the power of Junus and Jambrus everything was made. It was as though Aaron himself did it, but if Junus and Jambrus had not been present, then the calf would not

have been made. These two caused it to be made because they performed their magic and uttered their in-
cantations.

It is written, "When Aaron saw it [the calf] he built
an altar before it." How great was his desire for good,
but he did not know how to guard himself. As soon as
he cast the gold into the fire, the negative power became strengthened. As it is written, "And Aaron saw
it," meaning that he immediately saw the strengthen-
ing of the negative power, "and he built an altar before
it." Had he not hurried to do so, the world would have
again become a wasteland.

That is, the spiritual system would have been undone and replaced
by chaos.

So when Aaron saw that the negative side was becoming stronger, he grasped for a remedy. He strengthened
the holy side by building the altar. As soon as the negative power became aware of this image of the king
standing before it, its strength diminished and it re-
treated.

Just as darkness cannot exist in the presence of light, the negative
power evaporated before the holy altar that Aaron constructed.
Darkness and light do not compete. One simply cancels out the
other.

Then Aaron proclaimed, "Tomorrow shall be a feast to
the Creator," and not to the calf. He labored for the
side of holiness, and brought the people to the side of
holiness. This is the remedy that he brought forth. Had

he not done this, then the world would have come to an end. Still, the Creator's anger was aroused against Aaron, even though he did not intend any evil. The Creator said to him, "Aaron, these two sorcerers drew you toward what they wanted. By your life, two of your sons shall die because of this sin."

Aaron was caught between authentic long-term interests and the immediate demands of the moment. His solution was to enter a kind of gray area: He sought to relieve the pressure that had been placed on him, while intending to transfer responsibility to someone else. Aaron did not really lead the people in a proactive sense; he played for time. Hoping to be saved before it was too late, he offered the Egyptians concessions that he actually had no intention of fulfilling. This, rather than standing strong with certainty in the Creator both in his heart and on his lips.

Aaron had thought that in the meantime Moses would return, and therefore Moses did not destroy the altar that Aaron made. If it were as some people think— that he built the altar to honor the calf—then Moses should have immediately smashed the altar. But it happened quite differently, as it is written, "And he took the calf that they made and burned it and ground it into powder." And it does not say, "He smashed the altar." For it is written, "Moses saw the calf and the dancing," but the altar is not mentioned. Because Aaron knew that, "He who sacrifices to any god but the Creator shall be destroyed." Aaron was saved by the good plan he devised, which was done with no evil intention.

When the Creator judges the world, he judges it according to the majority of people. When Adam sinned by eating the fruit of the Tree of Knowledge, he caused Malchut [the physical realm], to become the dwelling place of death. . . . And this remained so until the children of Israel stood at Mount Sinai. When Israel stood at Mount Sinai, that curse of death was removed. But when Israel sinned with the calf, then the curse again became as before.

From the Zohar's perspective, few transgressions are as grievous as they seem, given a literal interpretation of the Bible: "Woe to any who see in the Law only simple stories and ordinary words. . . ." Again and again the Zohar reminds us that the Bible is a coded document whose hidden meanings must be discovered and carefully interpreted.

The incident of the golden calf offers a dramatic case in point. After escaping slavery in Egypt and miraculously crossing the Red Sea, the Israelites arrived at the foot of Mount Sinai. But as we have pointed out, in the Zohar, "Egypt" does not refer to a political or geographical entity. "Egypt" is a coded representation of a spiritual condition. It denotes slavery to the physical world, bondage to the degenerate attractions of material reality, and estrangement from the real treasure and fulfillment, which is the Light of the Creator. Moses leading Israel out of Egypt is an allegorical rendition of a people's struggle to move beyond the enslavement of ego toward a new, more spiritually evolved reality. And the Zohar teaches us to recognize this same story in our own lives. Each of us is challenged by the seductive bondage of "Egypt," from which each of us must find the way to break free.

In the Torah narrative, Moses ascends Mount Sinai to commune with God and receive the Law. But when he does not return as anticipated—according to a kabbalistic interpretation, he is just six hours late!—the people renounce God and in their impatience demand the building of an idol, the golden calf. At that point Moses reappears. Discovering an orgiastic celebration of the "molten beast," he smashes the newly received tablets of the Law and punishes the idol worshippers.

While this is all quite straightforward in the Bible, the Zohar's elaboration and interpretation is much more complex. As always, understanding of a particular incident is inseparable from all that has come before, beginning with the story of Creation. Kabbalah teaches that when God gave form to the universe, He endowed it with ten levels of divine energy. All creation was suffused with the Light of the Creator—nothing of "the good" was absent or withheld, and no "darkness" was in any way present. Death did not exist, nor even the consciousness of death. In this Paradise, a much different dimension than we inhabit today, the Tree-of-Life reality prevailed.

When Adam and Eve partook of the forbidden fruit of the Tree of the Knowledge of Good and Evil, they and all who came after them were instantly cut off from Tree-of-Life reality. Access to the ten levels of divine energy was withdrawn and blocked. Instead, there was a new consciousness of pain and death derived from the Tree of Knowledge, and it was this consciousness that brought death into being. By succumbing to the temptation of the serpent, they lost knowledge of the ultimate value of the spirit, and the material world—literally, the dust—now became the focus of their lives. The Creator Himself gave voice to this condemnation.

Genesis 3:17–19

Cursed be the ground because of you;
By toil shall you eat of it
All the days of your life:
Thorns and thistles shall it sprout for you.

But your food shall be the grasses of the field;
By the sweat of your brow
Shall you get bread to eat,
Until you return to the ground—
For from it you were taken.
For dust you are,
And to dust you shall return.

Moses' great achievement was to restore access to Tree-of-Life reality in the minds and hearts of his people. As always, the Torah expresses this allegorically. When Moses called down the ten plagues on the Egyptians, this represented a burning away of the spiritual barriers that had come into being with the sin of Adam. The plagues were a cleansing process that opened the way for a reconnection with Tree-of-Life reality. Immortality consciousness began to be restored. Certainty—an important word for Kabbalah—in the power of spirit over matter was regained. It was this certainty that made the crossing of the Red Sea possible.

At the foot of Mount Sinai, the *tikkun,* or spiritual correction, made necessary by the sin of Adam had been almost achieved with the escape from Egypt. The spiritual circuitry was close to regaining its original perfection. Instead, the loss of certainty, or trust, allowed mortality consciousness to reassert itself, leading to the creation of the golden idol.

If we were to identify a spiritual enemy or adversary to the spiritual progress of humankind in this world, it would be more accurate kabbalistically to call it *chaos* rather than evil. Chaos refers to disruption of the precisely ordered circuitry that exists between the physical realm and the Upper Worlds. The true purpose of humanity in general, and of every human being, is to connect with the Light of the Creator in greater and greater intensity, and eventually to literally *become one* with the Light. But creating this connection with the Light is not simply a matter of gaining access to it. Making ourselves ready to receive the Light means "preparing the vessel" into which the Light will flow. It means taking positive action in the everyday conduct of our lives, and observing the rituals and practices that the Creator has provided as tools for our transformation. It means replacing desire to receive for ourselves alone with desire to receive in order to share, and loving others as we love ourselves. As the great sage Hillel said, "The rest is commentary."

According to kabbalistic teachings, past incarnations determine the level of desire experienced by each of us. We are born with a certain degree of raw longing that does not increase or diminish throughout each lifetime, but our level of desire is always congruent with our authentic spiritual needs. Desire is the engine of movement and action. Individuals born with a greater degree of desire have more spiritual ground to make up, so to speak, and therefore they feel compelled to move more quickly than others. Why then, as frequently happens, do certain individuals who are born with intense needs fail to achieve their full potential, while others of lower intensity seem to prosper? The kabbalists find the cause in their ability to transform desire to receive for themselves alone into desire to receive in order to share.

How this plays over the course of a whole lifetime varies from person to person, but a whole lifetime is generally required. A close reading of the Zohar suggests that patience is absolutely essential. When things go wrong—when the circuitry of the Creator's Light is disrupted and chaos is introduced—it is very often a case of "too much too soon." Kabbalistic commentaries on the sin of Adam, for example, interpret the eating of the forbidden fruit from the Tree of Knowledge as a code for precipitous sexual "knowing" of Eve. Similarly, the golden calf came about through a loss of trust in the Creator, and a consequent connection with a destructive form of energy. The people wanted a god, and their loss of faith in Moses and the Creator caused them to fall back on their old ways of drawing strength. There are tempting ways to illicitly gain access to the power, and within our souls this stolen current may produce a sudden bright flash, as when a light bulb flares out. The ecstatic worship of the golden calf was such a flash. But darkness quickly follows, with much spiritual repair needing to be done.

Kabbalistically, a golden calf is really a captivating machine that helps us retreat to a comfortable refuge rather than face the trials presented by real growth. Anyone who has spent any time around young children has seen the phenomenon of "two steps forward, one step back." As a small child develops physically, mentally, and emotionally, the very progress itself can seem frightening. Advances in capability are frequently followed by regressions to earlier forms of behavior. While this is an understandable and even a useful behavior mechanism in children, it can be extremely counterproductive—though by no means uncommon—later in life.

Let us not underestimate the attractions of golden calves. They can be very exciting to play with. The Zohar teaches that the biblical golden calf could walk, talk, dance, and even change its shape. Today's version may come in the form of a car, a piece of jewelry, or a powerful new computer with instant Internet access. Golden calves are usually sleek and shiny. It's hard to take our eyes off them—which is really the problem, because they distract us from the Creator as the true source of Light, and from ourselves as the Vessel for which the Light is intended.

In today's world, advanced technology confronts us with many of the same challenges and opportunities that the golden calf presented to the people of Israel. On the one hand, we now possess instruments that give us astonishing powers. But this very strength, dramatically in evidence whenever we search the Internet or send an e-mail, can cause us to doubt or forget an even more startling reality: that we ourselves are capable of everything the most powerful computer can accomplish, and more. We literally have the power of immortality within our grasp. Therefore we ought not stand so much in awe of a machine's ability to quickly process information. We ought not cede to any technology the responsibility for fully developing ourselves on the spiritual plane. This, after all, is what took place at the time of the golden calf. It was not only that the people had grown impatient with waiting. They were also frightened of the opportunity that lay before them, and of accepting the responsibilities that came with it. So they found a way out. They "downloaded" everything into a magical object.

The results, it is fair to say, were quite disastrous. The possibility of reentering the Garden of Eden receded and vanished. It had really existed at Mount Sinai, but now it would again remain hidden.

Yet, what was at the root of this missed opportunity? Unbelievably, a simple lack of patience. Because what, after all, is patience? Just the unshakable knowledge—the certainty—that what is in our best interest will come to be. Certainty, trust, or, in this instance patience allows us to repel all doubt and stay the course during times of difficulty rather than seek or create poor substitutes for the Light.

CHAPTER 22

DAVID AND BATSHEVA

David is a uniquely human figure among the biblical patriarchs, closest to ourselves both chronologically and emotionally. As the youthful conqueror of Goliath, poet of the psalms, and king of Israel, he might have been a conventionally heroic personality. Yet Kabbalah teaches that David represents *Malchut*, the physical realm that we all inhabit. He seems to be subject to all the positive and negative influences that accompany human existence, and to the failings that result. Very significantly, however, this was his choice, not his destiny. The Zohar teaches that David's soul was by nature immune to all negativity. He could have chosen to remain above the conflicts of the human heart, but he asked the Creator to test him, even though this would cause him to transgress. As the Zohar puts it:

Vol. 3, p. 70

David said to the Creator, "Master of the Universe, why is there no blessing that ends with my name, as there is for Abraham?" The Creator answered David, "As for Abraham, I have already tried and tested him, and he resisted the test and was found before me to be wholly steadfast." Then David said to Him, "Try me, then, and test me."

By undertaking this challenge, David elevated his soul above pure righteousness to the higher category of sincere repentance. Though no longer a paragon, David exemplifies the supreme spiritual opportunity that comes with apparent failure. The Bible succinctly describes how David's test began:

II Samuel 11:1–6

Late one afternoon, David rose from his couch and strolled on the roof of the royal palace; and from the roof he saw a woman bathing. The woman was very beautiful, and the king sent someone to make inquiries about the woman. He reported, "She is Batsheva daughter of Eliam and the wife of Uriah the Hittite. David sent messengers to fetch her; she came to him and he lay with her—she had just purified herself after her period—and she went back home. The woman conceived, and she sent word to David, "I am pregnant." Thereupon David sent a message to Joab, "Send Uriah the Hittite to me"; and Joab sent Uriah to David.

When Uriah appeared before him, David commanded the Hittite to return to his home, knowing that upon a man's return from a journey or from battle, it was customary to make love to his wife. When Batsheva's pregnancy became known, David reasoned, her child would then be ascribed to her husband. But Uriah refused, preferring to remain on duty with his men. Therefore, when Uriah returned to the battlefront, David sent with him a sealed letter for Joab, the commander of the army. The letter directed that Uriah should be placed in a particularly dangerous area of the battle, and then abandoned. This was done, and Uriah was killed. And David married Batsheva.

Vol. 2, pp. 447–448

Rabbi Aba asked: "If Batsheva belonged to King David from the day the world was created, why did the Creator give her first to Uriah the Hittite?" Rabbi Shimon told him that these are the ways of the Creator. Although a woman may be destined to become a certain man's wife, another man may marry her first. But as soon as the time has come for the destined man to marry her, the latter is removed from this world, because of the other that comes after him. And it is very hard and painful for the Creator to remove that person from the world before his time has come.

Come and behold: Even though David confessed his sins and repented, he was not able to completely forget and extirpate them from his heart, especially the sin related to Batsheva. Because he always feared that one of his sins might reappear and persecute him in time of danger, he never forgot them or blotted them out of his memory. He said, "For I know my transgression, and my sin is before me always."

Remember: David could have avoided this peril if he had not explicitly asked God to tempt him. From a historical perspective, this is an extremely unusual depiction of an ancient hero. In the first book of the *Iliad,* Achilles prays—but certainly not for temptation. He prays for glory in battle. As a child, Alexander the Great wept at his father's military successes, worried that no nations would be left for him to conquer. Fifteen hundred years later, Genghis Khan sought out wizards and shamans—but he wanted to learn how to live forever, not how to elevate his soul.

To explain David's yearning for a test, even one that he would fail, we must understand the Zohar's depiction of the patriarchs and matriarchs. Remember that on the one hand, these biblical characters experienced life as flesh-and-blood individuals who were born, ate, slept, worked, loved, and died. At the same time, they were deeply aware of their role as collaborators with God in the work of creation. They were partners also in the creation of the biblical narrative that is an encoded guidebook—a template— for drawing ever closer to the Creator. When David asks God to test him, he is in effect asking to be made a *better character* in the Bible. He wants greater scenes, more dramatic lines, because he knows this will elevate both himself and the story, and he knows this will help all of us who come after him. He chooses tragedy, because tragedy can engender contrition and redemption—and it is these qualities that David literally makes possible for the rest of us.

The Zohar is explicit about the difference between righteousness and repentance: the latter is a much higher spiritual category. In the complex hierarchy of merit that comprises the Upper Worlds, the Zohar places the souls of repentant sinners well above those of people who were merely good. Even people who had intended to repent, but who died before they got a chance, receive credit for their good intentions. Moreover, the Creator takes great pains to provide opportunities for repentance. This is why the wicked are not immediately punished for their sins. God delays executing judgment against them, often for the full duration of their lives, because an evil person who repents brings more Light into the world than a multitude of exemplary citizens. And in the world to come the souls of the righteous may have to wait years before entering into the presence of God, but the penitent gain this blessing immediately.

Indeed, the Zohar teaches the true "purpose" of evil is to foster repentance. Otherwise, why doesn't God simply eliminate evil from creation altogether? *It is to give us the opportunity to take full responsibility for our own elevation and growth.* When we succumb to evil tendencies, repentance allows us to restore the Light we have lost. And as always, what occurs in the life of any individual immediately reverberates throughout the world and through all Creation. Therefore a contrite soul brings Light into the physical realm and joy to the inhabitants of the Upper Worlds.

According to kabbalistic teaching, whatever is most difficult is also most highly valued, and to sincerely repent for a misguided action is one of the most challenging and rewarding activities of the human heart.

The difficulty that many experience with regard to repentance is usually attributed to pride, or to fear of acknowledging that we have really done something that is not in accord with the image we would like to have of our self. But what is often overlooked is the seductiveness and even the pleasure of holding onto guilt. Kabbalah, therefore, doesn't emphasize the value of repentance as an aspect of goodness. Repentance is important because the alternative of guilt can be so subtly and powerfully alluring. In addition, the energy of repentance has an affinity with the Light that transcends ethical considerations. More than a question of morality, it is a kind of magnetism.

In any case, there is no doubt that David was very contrite: His sin remained, in his own words, "before my eyes every day of my life." It is said that he even contracted leprosy for a time, whereby physical suffering could match his spiritual pain. But there is a happy ending. The biblical commentaries make it clear that David's redemption is ultimately fulfilled.

On the Day of Judgment, God will prepare a banquet in Heaven. At the end of the banquet, He will offer a cup of wine to the patriarch Abraham with these words: "Pronounce the blessing over the wine, you who are the father of the pious people of the world!" But Abraham will decline, saying, "I am also the father of the people of Ishmael, who kindle God's wrath."

God will then offer the cup to Isaac: "Pronounce the blessing, you who were bound to the altar as a sacrifice!" But Isaac will reply, "I am not worthy, because the descendants of my son Esau destroyed the Temple."

God will turn to Jacob: "Give the blessing, for your children were blameless!" But Jacob will refuse, for he transgressed by marrying two sisters at the same time. Even Moses will decline to bless the wine, since he was found unworthy to enter the land of Canaan.

Finally God will pass the cup to David: "Pronounce the blessing, for you were the sweetest singer in Israel, and also Israel's king!" Then David will take the cup and reply, "Yes, I will give the blessing, for I am worthy of the honor. I have sinned, and I have repented, and my sin and the sins of others have been washed away." Whereupon God will send his angels to open the gates of hell and admit the condemned souls to Paradise.

CHAPTER 23

SOUL MATES

Kabbalah describes the creation of the world as an ongoing process at every level of being. Collectively, humanity is moving toward the day when suffering and death disappear, and we regain the Tree-of-Life reality that was intended for us. Individually, too, we are works in progress. Each of us came to this world to achieve specific spiritual goals that will culminate in our achieving oneness with God. In this endeavor there is no such thing as failure. Our transformation is ordained and assured by the Creator. How long it takes depends entirely on us.

But why does it have to be so *hard*? Why doesn't God just make it all happen right now? In Virgil's *Aeneid*, the god of the sea stretches forth his trident, and a raging storm instantly becomes calm. Surely the true Creator of the universe can do as much against the storms of many kinds that assail us. What is He waiting for?

The comparison with classical mythology can be illuminating. In the *Iliad*, the gods cast lots to determine men's fate. But Kabbalah teaches that we are partners with the Creator, not His puppets. Even God Himself cannot simply wave a magic wand and "give" us the transformation of our souls. We need to earn that transformation. We must *merit* it. And that requires a great deal of spiritual work.

Once again, our ultimate goal is oneness with the nature of God: the transformation of the desire to receive for the self alone into desire to receive for the purpose of sharing. Toward this objective, the Zohar emphasizes the importance of an extraordinary category of human relationship. In Hebrew, it is called *Ben Zug* in the male form and *Bat Zug* in the female. It is usually translated in English as *soul mate*.

Soul mates are two halves of a single soul, divided by the Creator Himself in the supernal realm. As the correction (*tikkun*) of our spiritual selves is accomplished in our lifetime, or as we at least work diligently toward achieving that correction, the Creator makes us whole again.

None of it is easy. Not for us, and not even for Him. In fact, an authentic soul-mate relationship can be known at least by part in the difficulties that attend it. The sages taught that a man's soul mate must travel across an ocean to reach him. As always with Kabbalah we should avoid a merely literal understanding of this. The expanse to be crossed may be one of language, social class, or physical distance, but obstacles are part of the experience of soul-mate bonding.

As a psychological and emotional principle, poets have always understood this. From the plays of William Shakespeare to Erich Segal's *Love Story*, problems in love have been portrayed as evidence of its promise. Stendhal, in his taxonomy of romance entitled *On Love*, refers to a seeming "unattainability" as the first requirement for deep intimate connection. The obstacles that arise between soul mates, as emotional experience in the physical world, are not the sum of the experience. They are reflections of the fundamentally spiritual process that soul-mate reunion represents.

As I write about these teachings at the start of the twenty-first century, it strikes me that aspects of them may seem out of synch with the times, if not actually retrograde. The valorization of diffi-

Soul Mates 225

culty in an emotional relationship? A psychotherapist might call this masochism rather than spirituality. And there is more. Kabbalah is anything but politically correct on the topic of men and women. The sages, for example, tell us that the soul-mate enterprise is fundamentally a male undertaking. It is *he* who must begin spiritual work in order to make reunification possible. *His* spiritual progress creates the requisite energy.

It is in the nature of things that women accomplish their *tikkun* with less difficulty than men. In a tradition that celebrates profound struggle to overcome adversity, including the attributes of an individual's nature, this seemingly translates to a subordinate or, more accurately, supportive feminine role. Kabbalah teaches that most women come into the world to help men move toward the spiritual correction that they find so much more difficult. The harridan, the termagant, the battle ax, the shrew—kabbalists explain that these women are doing exactly what they should be doing for (or to) their husbands. They are helping them achieve their *tikkun*.

Yet this is not to say that women are in any way second-class citizens. In fact, they come from the sefirotic level of *Binah*, which endows them with great spiritual potential. A more accurate designation would be "power beside the throne"—an extremely important position in Kabbalah. Abraham Lincoln was a great man, perhaps a *tzaddik*, a spark of the ancient patriarch Abraham, with whom he quite consciously identified. But Kabbalah would give credit equal to Mary Todd.

Vol. 3, pp. 187–191

Souls that are destined to come into the world appear before Him as pairs, each soul divided into male and female halves.

Just as God exists beyond male and female, so too did we in the Upper Worlds. There, as in the cells of the microscopic human embryo, creation begins with division. We are split off from our primordial wholeness—physically, spiritually, and in our gender identity.

The Zohar describes the gender separation process in some detail.

> Happy are the righteous, whose souls are adorned as they appear in front of the Creator before coming to this world. When the Creator sends them into the world, all these souls include a male and a female joined together.
>
> They are handed over to a governor, whose name is Lailah (Eng. "Night"), who oversees human conception. When the souls descend into the world and are handed over to the governor, they are separated from one another. Sometimes one precedes the other in coming down and entering the body of a human being.

By embarking on a spiritual path, and by following that path through the twists and turns of a lifetime, we can merit return to our former unity. We can gain the ultimate joining together, not with another person, but with the lost part of ourselves.

The kabbalists explain that this happens in a number of ways, some of them quite miraculous. Because women tend to complete their spiritual correction sooner and more easily than men, they are also more often freed from the cycle of birth, death, and rebirth required of those who have not yet achieved their *tikkun*. A woman's soul, therefore, may have the privilege of residing in the Upper Worlds while her male soul mate must reenter the world. However, she may so strongly wish to assist him in his efforts toward correction that she voluntarily comes into the physical dimension. She reincarnates to become the wife of her soul mate. He must merit her presence, however. Many lifetimes may pass before this is the case, but it is worth the wait. In fact, Kabbalah teaches that the re-unification of soul mates is a greater miracle than the parting of the Red Sea.

> When their time to be married arrives, the Creator who knows these spirits and souls joins them as they were before they came into the world. When they are joined together, they become one body and one soul, right and left in proper unison. As it is written, "There is nothing new under the sun," because this is nothing new but a return to how they were before coming down to this world.
>
> You might say, "But we have learned that a man ob-tains a mate according to his deeds and his behavior." It is assuredly so! If he is meritorious and his ways are correct, then he deserves his own soul mate, to join her as they were joined when they left the Creator, and be-fore bonding with a physical body.

Nothing that takes place in the physical dimension is more cele-brated by Kabbalah than the joining of soul mates, and toward that end almost any hardship or sacrifice is permissible. If a married man and a married woman recognize one another as two halves of the same soul, they must divorce their spouses in order to be together—and their spouses must willingly let them go in order to fulfill the higher spiritual purpose. And the stakes can go much higher. In the biblical story of David and his soul mate Batsheva, Batsheva's husband Uriah even had to die in order to clear the way for the reunification. This was not for a sentimental purpose, as in a romance novel, but to bring the future people of Israel into the physical plane as their descendants.

Clearly, a great many complexities can arise, and the Zohar deals with a number of them. Imagine a good man who, by diligently pursuing a spiritual path, merits a good wife, although not yet his true soul mate. Imagine also, then, that *her* soul mate appears on the scene. Unfortunately, the marriage must end—and if the husband realizes this and acts accordingly, perhaps he will merit his own soul mate before long. Another example might be that either the man or the woman in a relationship believes the other is his or her soul mate, while, for whatever reason, the other harbors doubts that they are divinely matched. This is not a matter that can be settled arbitrarily or based upon "feelings." On the material plane we often are misguided by our emotions. Over time the truth of the matter will emerge through events, and that truth may be surprising to both partners.

Like Darwinian natural selection, the joining of soul mates is a force that cannot be denied. Nor should anyone try to deny it, since the Light brought to the world by reunited soul mates hugely benefits all. From the point of view of the soul mates themselves, there is a key recognition factor: an awareness of the Light they can reveal to the world. Soul-mate bonding is not about birds twittering in the trees. The relationship may not be a smooth one in conventional terms. But there is an absolutely clear realization by both the man and the woman that they were meant to be together, not just for their own well-being, but for what they can bring to the world.

It is interesting that the Zohar's discussion of soul-mate bonding concludes with an encomium to another profound relationship— that of each individual to the Torah.

> Happy is the portion of Israel, because the Torah teaches them the ways of conduct of the Creator, as

well as all His secrets and the mysteries hidden before Him.

Indeed, it is written, "The Torah of the Creator is perfect." Happy is the portion of Him who studies Torah and is never separated from it. Because whoever abandons the Torah, even for one moment, is separated from eternal life. Therefore it is written, "For it is your life and the length of your days, and length of days and years of life and peace it shall add to you."

Remember that Torah study does not refer to a close reading of the Five Books of Moses as they are printed on a page. In this context, study means opening a channel to divine wisdom. Torah study is the way of life that reveals Light in the world, and that unites us with the sharing essence of the Creator. Whenever we perform an act of true sharing, or even sincerely desire to perform such an act, we are "studying" Torah in this sense. As you recall, Torah literally means "truth." Whenever we hold the Torah close to our hearts as we would our soul mate, we add "length of days" to our own lives and we hasten the end of suffering and death for all humanity. It is not an accident that the Zohar's discussion of soul mates ends with invocation of the Torah. These two intimate relationships illuminate one another. Both depict a love grounded in the everyday world, but whose origins are in the realm of the infinite.

CHAPTER 24

WHY THE WICKED ARE SO STRONG

I f the Creator is good, why do the wicked prosper, and why
are the righteous everywhere afflicted? Why do a relatively
small number of people have more wealth than they can
ever use, while many people in the world have barely enough to survive on? Perhaps most disturbing of all, why does it seem that the
good not infrequently die young, while the less than good live to a
ripe old age?

In confronting these questions, the Zohar begins with the assumption that answers cannot be found in the material world. We
must recognize the existence of another dimension of being in
order to integrate our perceptions of manifest injustice with our understanding of the existence of a just God. The sages of Kabbalah,
therefore, show no interest in analyzing the material foundations of
injustice, or of trying to alter these foundations at the level of material reality. While *tzedakah* (charity) is an important kabbalistic
tool, Kabbalah's focus is on the spiritual benefits to the giver rather
than any effects on the circumstances of the recipient.

In this sense, Kabbalah is an ancient philosophy, although
"timeless" would be a better word. In the context of human history,
it is only a moment ago that injustice came to be seen as something
other than a natural force, and that resisting it seemed wise or even

possible. Neither Moses nor Buddha nor Jesus preached attack on the societal order, no matter how oppressive. For the kabbalists, even the escape from Egypt is understood as a spiritual allegory rather than a revolution. The goal was freedom, but freedom in the sense of transcendence: a chance to ascend closer to the Upper Worlds, not to create a better life in this one.

Today, when people want change, they want it in three dimensions, not ten, and they want it while they are still breathing. Heaven can wait. "We live in a material world" was not just the refrain of a popular song; it is the axiom upon which our society's intentions are built, whether expressed by the New Deal or Compassionate Conservatism.

The extreme form of materialist economic analysis, of course, is Marxism, and it may be useful for a moment to contrast this with the pure spirituality of Kabbalah, which is Marxism's mirror image. To be sure, Kabbalah is a revolutionary teaching. Kabbalists share the revolutionary materialist's apocalyptic goal of creating an environment of perfect harmony for humanity—but only as the end, not the means to the end. A materialist rejects anything outside a material solution to injustice, not to mention evil. It takes wisdom to be able to recognize the exploitation of one person, or one class, by another when that exploitation is well hidden or disguised. To the materialist, wise action means taking sides with the class that has history on its side.

A materialist, therefore, admires the wisdom that Kabbalah ascribes to the Creator: the power to see the end in the beginning. But "beginning" for a materialist means the point in time when work came into being, Genesis 3:19 at the earliest; and "end" in the materialist context means the establishment of a just society. The beginning for Kabbalah, however, is the primordial environment of the Light and the Vessel, before matter itself came into being. The end is not just the eradication of injustice, but the end of time itself.

Until that transcendent occasion, Kabbalah and the Zohar explain the presence of human suffering not in material terms, but through a moral and spiritual calculus. For example, what we might look upon as an untimely death might actually be an intervention, a rescue mission by the Creator on behalf of the worthy.

Vol. 8, pp. 93–97

> Two things cause the righteous to leave the world before their time. First, because of the sins of their generation; when the wicked multiply in the world, the righteous who are among them are caught in their sins. Second, when it is revealed before the Holy One, blessed be He, that they will sin later on. He then removes them from the world before their time. . . . They are treated as though they had sinned by celestial justice.

When the number of the wicked among us at a particular place and time becomes overwhelming, even the good people fall under their influence, as if by the gravitational pull of a very large, high-density mass. This is a very important kabbalistic idea, analogous to the concept of critical mass in physics. Just as we share the air we breathe, we share in the condition of one another's souls. Spiritually as well as physically, we take in what is all around us. When a sufficiently extreme environment of negative energy is established, even the good are compelled to participate in it. They also suffer the consequences, as with the early death discussed here. On other occasions, when the Creator sees this critical

mass is about to be reached, He removes the righteous souls pe-
remptorily.

> Did not Solomon say, "There are just men to whom it
> happens according to the deeds of the wicked"? They
> are judged from above as though they sinned and acted
> like the wicked. Also, there are wicked men to whom it
> happens according to the deeds of the righteous. They
> sit quietly and peacefully in the world and judgment
> does not reach them, as though they had acted like
> righteous people.
>   Why does it thus happen to the wicked according to
> the deeds of the righteous? Because it may be revealed
> to the Holy One, blessed be He, that the wicked will
> repent. Or it may be that a righteous person will de-
> scend from them, as with Terach, from whom emanated
> the true seed of Abraham.

There is injustice on the level of our experience and perception,
just as there are colors and seasons in the natural world. But
the Creator—and truly righteous human souls—understands that
seeming injustice is only the inability to see the bigger picture.
Again and again Kabbalah and the Zohar confront *apparent* mis-
takes, whether in the sacred texts or in the business of living. Again
and again the problem is reframed in a larger, spiritual context, and
thereby resolved. Things arc not wrong. They only appear that way
until, using the tools of Kabbalah, we resolve the contradictions
and see through the paradoxes.

> For we have learned that the Holy One, blessed be He,
> has made both righteous and wicked people in the

world. Just as he is honored in the world by the actions
of the righteous, so he is honored by the actions of the
wicked when they do good actions in the world. As it is
written: "He has made everything beautiful in its
time."

The somewhat startling point of this selection, that God is honored by the occasional good acts of bad people, is made even more
strongly elsewhere in the Zohar and in other kabbalistic teachings.
The Creator is not just *equally* pleased by the positive acts of the
righteous and the wicked. He is more pleased with the good deeds
of the wicked than He is with those to whom righteous acts come
more effortlessly. There is more joy in the Upper Worlds when a
sheep returns to the fold than when a sheep never strays in the first
place. In short, for Kabbalah, repentance is a higher spiritual category than righteousness.

Many new students find this difficult to accept. To understand
this important teaching, we must consider two distinct elements of
evil action: first, the impulse that gives rise to it, and then the debili-
tating effects of evil, not on those who are sinned against, but on
the sinners themselves.

Several times we have mentioned great writers and scientists
who have studied Kabbalah. It is unlikely that Oscar Wilde was one
of them, but when he wrote, "I can resist anything but temptation,"
Wilde was surprisingly close to a kabbalistic perspective on the
human soul. Kabbalah teaches that, at its origin, desire is always a
positive energy. All wanting, even the most self-serving or destructive, is a version (even if a distortion) of desire for the Light.

Desire, according to Kabbalah, stems from an inner longing that
has *already* attained and experienced its ultimate fulfillment. "It is
impossible for any Desire to be stirred up in Existence unless at a

previous time a fulfillment was revealed sufficient to that Desire,"
wrote Rabbi Isaac Luria: "Desire in the Upper Worlds becomes potential and a necessity in the Lower Worlds."

Any physical effect is initiated by a cause on the metaphysical
plane. As the Endless World was the cause of everything, it follows
that it also encompassed every desire and every fulfillment that was,
is, or ever will be. Every desire we may have is already fulfilled in the
Upper World; every wish has already been granted. Kabbalah
teaches that fulfillment *precedes* desire, and that every effect is contained within its cause.

Those who have known intense desire may have fallen, but they
have also evinced the "raw material" of transformation. They may
have taken a wrong turn, they may even be going completely in the
wrong direction, but they are at least on the road. Another analogy?
A person who sins is like a poorly wired house. Short circuits and
even fires may occur, but there is nothing wrong with the power
supply.

Perhaps it seems that whenever we talk about the mechanics of
Kabbalah we are using the jargon of electricians. Truthfully, since
what we are dealing with is the idea of channeling and transforming energy, and receiving greater or lesser amounts of Light, there
are few other fields in our material world that so well lend themselves to comparison. But let me offer one more analogy not drawn
from that context: The Light of the Creator, like nature in general,
abhors a vacuum. A person who is spiritually empty can be a powerful attractor of the Light, once even a tiny entranceway presents
itself.

The idea that a great sinner has the potential to become a righteous person exists in many spiritual traditions, but a second reason
for the high regard given sinners' positive actions is unique to Kabbalah. The kabbalists tell us that the negative force can assume

many disguises: as the Torah puts it, "The serpent was more subtle than any other beast of the field that the Creator had made." When a person has behaved badly, or perhaps even led a truly evil life, redemption may seem impossible. An inner voice says, "You've gone too far. The harm you've done outweighs any good you could possibly accomplish. There is not enough time left. You're a condemned soul, so just accept it." This may seem like a version of humility, or at least honesty, but Kabbalah recognizes such thoughts as just a subtle expression of ego and self-absorption. Psychoanalysis calls it narcissism, an addiction to ourselves as we are, and it is a powerful impediment to real change.

The Zohar's elevation or even celebration of repentance is intended to confront this reverse egotism. By assuring us that the door to transformation is always open, even at life's final moment, Kabbalah asserts that it is never too late to change. By teaching that later (or greater) change is most joyfully welcomed by the Upper Worlds, the Zohar intends to disarm the negative inclination of one of its most potent weapons. Resignation to one's fate has no place in kabbalistic teaching. The voice that tells us to give up hope is never the voice of wisdom. It is only the evil inclination broadcasting on an alternate frequency.

Kabbalah does not teach us to forget the past, but it does urge us to concentrate on the future. It does not ignore evil that may have been done, but it focuses our attention on the good that we can yet do.

Unless we are able to see the big picture—see the end in the beginning as the Creator does—it can appear to us that the evil in the world is overwhelming relative to the good. But this is simply an illusion, an unenlightened view of things. Evil exists in this world solely to provide opportunities for transformation. It is futile to attempt to combat or "transform" evil itself by addressing it "head on." We only can dispel it by doing our spiritual work quite literally in spite of evil. Evil is not really an opposite force to good, much less an equal one. Evil is simply the absence of good, as darkness is the absence of light. Once light appears, darkness is utterly gone. There is no residue of darkness in a room once the light has been turned on. This is as true on the spiritual level as it is in the physical world.

CHAPTER 25

IMMORTALITY

In scientific research, a distinction is sometimes made between "hard" and "soft" versions of an idea or hypothesis. Physicists, for example, refer to hard and soft interpretations of the so-called anthropic principle, which deals with the relationship between life, consciousness, and physical reality. The soft version asserts that life and consciousness came into being because the universe is precisely calibrated to make this possible. The hard version turns this on its head: Consciousness itself brought the universe into being, rather than the other way around.

A similar hard/soft distinction exists in spiritual matters, and this is especially clear in regard to immortality. Most religions and even many secular thinkers profess belief in some form of existence after death. A "soft" version of this belief might assert that we live on in the memories of our survivors, or in the lasting effects of the good and bad actions we performed in the world. A "harder" approach might suggest that our souls survive the death of the physical body: that they continue to exist in another dimension, and perhaps even participate in the world in some disembodied form. But only the "hardest" version of immortality would suggest that even our physical bodies and our individual identities can live on forever. This, in fact, is exactly what Kabbalah teaches.

This most revolutionary transformation will come about

through a combination of scientific and spiritual breakthroughs, although the distinction between those two categories is rapidly breaking down. Near-death experiences, for example, have received the attention of both physicians and clergy, calling on each other to help explain a phenomenon that essentially mystifies both camps. It is a fact, however, that in modern hospitals patients who have been declared clinically dead actually return to life. It is also a fact that we have been conditioned to doubt this, or to soften our interpretation, by what we have been told is a "scientific" view of what is possible and what is not. This conditioning toward doubt has been going on for a very long time. It began in the Garden of Eden, and our first instructor in the limits of possibility was none other than the serpent himself. One of Kabbalah's most important teachings states that negative thoughts are the origin of chaos in our lives. And of all negative thoughts, doubt may be the deadliest.

Kabbalah teaches that chaos—and death, which is the supreme manifestation of chaos—are illusions fostered by doubt, which creates an opening for negative energy. More specifically, doubt is a questioning of the efficiency—or the existence—of the spiritual system. It is doubt of oneself, and of one's own ability to reveal Light. While we still existed under the influence of Tree-of-Life consciousness—before the serpent instigated the tasting of the fruit from the Tree of Knowledge of Good and Evil—death did not exist. Humanity had no connection with "mortality consciousness." But once the fruit was eaten, uncertainty entered the picture. That is, we now doubted that we would live forever, and consequently, we do not live forever. It is the doubt itself that brought us the seeming "reality" of death. When humanity is at last transformed, all chaos, including death, will cease to exist. These burdens will evanesce like the Cheshire cat, vanishing into thin air.

To new students of Kabbalah, this must surely seem a radical assertion, and perhaps even an incredible one. Let us, therefore, look more closely at Kabbalah's explanation of exactly how chaos and death become a presence in our lives, and how they can be erased.

When a new life comes into being as a fertilized egg in the womb, this quite obviously represents the beginning of a process, but it is also the completion of a prior chain of events. Male and female energies have joined to form a single cell that encompasses both elements. In this state of wholeness, Kabbalah teaches that the cell is absolutely safe from negative influence. Moreover, surrounded by amniotic fluid, it is protected yet again, in accordance with the kabbalistic teaching that immersion in water provides a shield that chaos cannot penetrate. This condition of utter invulnerability is short-lived, however. The growth process begins, and new cells become differentiated as organs, connective tissues, or thousands of other possibilities. Differentiation, of course, is a necessary and positive development, but it also represents a loss of the completeness that characterized the human cell in its undifferentiated form. By its very nature, the growth of the organism brings about openings in the once impenetrable shield. And when birth brings departure from the immersion within the womb, that protection is lost as well.

As life goes on, our loss of wholeness continues apace, and not always as a concomitant of healthy growth. Openings for negativity are created every minute of every day. This is the nature of the world in which we live, and the people we have become. It is also the cause of illness, aging, and death—and it has a fundamentally spiritual basis. The spiritual foundation of the body's deterioration and disease underlies all biomechanical and biochemical processes. These processes are effects, although they are often mistaken for causes.

Let me be more specific. When an action or thought affects another human being negatively, the person responsible for that effect increases the quantity of "negative entities" that are drawn toward his or her own being. Indeed, the responsible person alone created those entities. When we focus destructive energy on others, we bring into being the means of our own self-destruction. Nor is there any shield against these entities; since they are of our own making, they gain entrance to our innermost being as easily as a robber to whom we have handed our house keys.

Fortunately, the reverse of this process is also true. By using the tools of Kabbalah, and most especially the Zohar, we create positive forces whose very existence is inimical to the presence of negativity, just as light is inimical to darkness. The spiritual tools of Kabbalah are not just a defense mechanism. They are a means of rebirth, or even *pre*birth—a way of returning to the undifferentiated state that, for the individual, is analogous to the Tree-of-Life reality for humanity as a whole. If we find this difficult to accept, it is only because a materialist, mechanistic definition of reality has limited our sense of what is possible. But these limiting thoughts are the work of our Adversary, the Angel of Doubt. Know your opponent!

The teachings of Kabbalah are a way of life, encompassing action, feeling, and especially thought, which the Zohar particularly emphasizes. Misfortune, illness, and death can never be understood independently of the thoughts that were their seeds. In our minds and souls, we have the power to heal and the power to remain well. We also have the power to achieve immortality.

Regardless of what the Angel of Doubt would have you believe, physical immortality is a reality today, just as it was in the Garden. If immortality seems unavailable, it is because we have detached from the consciousness of infinity and become full citizens of the mundane. Here again the insights of science can be useful. In 1924, the great physicist Niels Bohr described a principle that he called *complementarity*. Bohr stated that when a phenomenon is observed in a particular way, the means of observation that reveals certain truths about the phenomenon can obscure other truths. The classic example is an experiment on the nature of light, in which the light's properties as a particle renders its wave properties invisible, and vice versa. If we think of our five senses as an experimental apparatus, the complementarity principle tells us that "what we see is what we get"—but there is more to be gotten that we don't see. In a similar way, the "exclusionary" principle described by Wolfgang Pauli in 1925 teaches that no two electrons in an atom can occupy the same energy state simultaneously. Pauli further believed that the principle can be extended to systems much larger than the atom.

From a kabbalistic perspective, I infer from this that the Tree-of-Life reality cannot coexist with the world we now live in, just as a room cannot be filled with light and darkness at the same time. Indeed, the dimension of the Tree of Life cannot even be perceived without a fundamental shift in our perceptions, and in the hidden expectations or doubts that exist within them. We do not "see" immortality because we have focused our awareness elsewhere. As the physicists tell us, consciousness appropriate to a dimension of reality is the prerequisite for accessing that dimension; therefore immortality consciousness is essential for understanding how immortality can be attained, and for acting on that understanding.

Man was created on the sixth day. Why was this very important creation saved for last? It is because humanity is the culmination of all that came before, not only in the world as we know it but in the universe as a whole. Kabbalah teaches that the universe is literally the extended body of humankind—a holographic representation of ourselves. Just as the human body consists of members and parts that form a single organism, so does the world at large consist of a hierarchy of created things, which act and react together to form an organic whole.

We are the blueprint of the entire cosmos, as well as participants in it. Nor are we only participants. Humanity was endowed by the Creator with the power to influence and determine the very nature of the universe, from the quantum level to the birth and death of stars. The instrument of this great power is nothing more than our consciousness, and our realization of the capabilities that are within our grasp. Kabbalah teaches that our thoughts, feelings, and especially our spiritual awareness determine events in the external environment. What takes place in our minds and hearts is the ground state of the physical realm. This view, it is interesting to note, is also expressed in the so-called Copenhagen interpretation theory of quantum mechanics, as articulated by Niels Bohr. Bohr's ideas also erase the clear-cut division between events, physical objects, and human consciousness. At the most basic level, what is observed cannot escape being influenced by whoever is observing. In fact, in the absence of an observer, what we think of as immutable physical reality does not even exist.

The Zohar depicts humankind as an essentially spiritual entity whose fate is determined by the nature of our own thoughts and actions. That is to say, it is all up to us. Only human beings have the power of free will in determining their spiritual evolution, which in turn is the controlling energy of their physical and material well-being. The fundamental interconnection of consciousness and creation is the very essence of the zoharic worldview. To perceive and embrace this unity is to experience the true spirit of Kabbalah.

Kabbalah teaches that the even the most basic foundations of the physical world have their origins in the metaphysical or spiritual dimension. This requires us to think of life and death in terms that perhaps cannot be quantified or measured by technological means, but that have their own kind of validity and reality. From this perspective, death is the offspring of aspects of the physical dimension such as gravity and entropy, as described by Maxwell's Second Law of Thermodynamics. The kabbalists tell us that the origin of these seemingly immutable forces is nothing more than the desire to receive for the self alone. When self-directed desire is transformed into desire to receive for the sake of sharing, both gravity and entropy will cease to exist—along with the limitations of time, space, and matter itself. Kabbalah is very clear about this: The only reason that aging, pain, and death are part of human experience is the control over the material universe exerted by the desire for ourselves alone. When that control is eliminated, all those "realities" will be erased.

Many centuries ago, Rabbi Shimon bar Yochai wrote that two thousand years would pass before the raising of human consciousness to a new level of awareness would become possible. That moment has finally arrived. A global transformation from greed to sharing is taking place as never before. When a critical mass of the world's peoples participates in this transformation, immortality will become a reality.

As these immense changes take place, the spiritual tools of Kabbalah can help us to strengthen the consciousness of immortality, as well as to understand its connection to the primordial events of the Genesis story. Specifically, the Zohar takes up the theme of immortality in a discussion of Adam's progeny.

Vol. 2, pp. 293–295

If Adam had brought generations with him from Eden, they all would have lived forever, and not even the angels above could have stood before them and borne their brilliance and wisdom. And the light of the moon would never have been darkened. As it is written: "In the image of Elohim did He create him." (Genesis 1:27) But because Adam was the cause of sin,

he had to leave Eden and bear children outside. Therefore his generations did not last.

Rabbi Chizkiyah asked: "How could they have begotten offspring in Eden? Had the evil inclination
[that is, the desire to receive for the self alone, which is
inherent to the physical body] not been drawn down
on him and enticed him to sin, he would have dwelled
alone in the world and not begotten any offspring!"

Rabbi Aba answered: "Had Adam not sinned, he
would not have borne offspring from the side of the
evil inclination, but he would have borne them from
the side of the Light. But because he produced offspring only from the side of the evil inclination, all the
offspring of mankind, who are the sons of Adam, are
also from the side of the evil inclination. They have no
permanent existence, because the Other Side has been
mixed with them."

Consider the Fall of Adam. It occurred in Paradise, in the
Garden of Eden. What kind of people were fit to live in Paradise?
What level of souls would be the internal correlative of a perfect
external environment? Quite logically, the answer is *perfect* souls,
which is what Adam and Eve were at the time of their creation.
Not perfect in the sense of pristinely delicate, like a porcelain cup
or a Swiss watch, but perfect in the exact harmony between what
was in Adam's heart and what surrounded his body. There was congruence. There was equilibrium. There was unity.

So far, this is the version of Adam and Eve in the Garden as
presented in the Bible and the talmudic commentaries. Kabbalah is
a coded description of metaphysical forces at work. Adam and Eve
are not just two people. They are a metaphor for the primordial
Vessel whose existence preceded creation. Just as all the colors of

the spectrum exist within a single beam of sunlight, the Vessel encompassed all matter, space, time, and consciousness. And all the souls of humankind were also present in the Vessel.

As we discussed in chapter 5 ("The Light of Desire"), the Vessel shattered because of a contradiction in its nature. It had been created only to receive, but, in being filled with the Creator's Light, it had also received and taken on a degree of the Creator's own nature: the desire to share. All of our existence now is predicated on the goal of transforming this duality into a single desire, the desire to receive for the sake of sharing, in order to be able to finally reconnect with the Creator and receive the fullness of His Light.

This can happen in only one way. The shards of the shattered Vessel—you and I—must choose to make it happen. We must choose of our own free will to transform ourselves into "beings of sharing," as the kabbalists say, first on an individual level, and ultimately as a collective transformation of all humankind. Not even God can do this for us. Transformation is the supreme expression and the only expression of free will. It is the choice we make in every thought, feeling, and action. Adam and Eve faced this choice in the Garden. They chose wrongly but, as we will see, their intentions were good.

No question in spirituality has ignited more evil behavior than the nature of evil itself. Wars have been fought and crusades have been mounted over how evil came into being and why it persists. Does it stand as an autonomous force separate and opposite to God? Or does evil, like everything else, come from God, and even serve Him in accordance with its nature?

Kabbalah takes the latter position. It is evil, represented by the serpent in the Genesis story, that makes the choice of good possible. The allure of evil also makes that choice more difficult, and therefore more worthy. Evil, in its way, therefore serves the Creator. Indeed, by understanding this we can free ourselves from its temptations. A parable in the Zohar dramatizes this teaching: A king forbade his son to consort with harlots, but then he hired a harlot to test the strength of his son's character. The son was tempted—until he realized that the harlot was acting in the service of his father. She then lost all her power over him.

The serpent in the Garden (acting in the service of *our* Father) is essential to our final transformation, but he certainly doesn't make it any easier! At the time of his fateful encounter with Adam and Eve at the Tree of Knowledge, their state of being was fundamentally different from what ours is now. They embodied the pure energy of desire, and Kabbalah teaches that desire is inherently a positive force. While the conventional view of our first ancestors portrays them as transgressors, the kabbalists point out that their motivation was to serve God. The serpent understood this also. In fact, he used their positive intentions to manipulate them for his own ends. He fostered the transformation of their pure, undifferentiated desire into desire to receive for themselves alone.

Genesis 3:4

And the serpent said to the woman, "You are not going to die, but God knows that as soon as you eat of [the tree] your eyes will be opened and you will be like divine beings who know good and bad."

Much kabbalistic teaching underlies the serpent's pronouncement. He refers to the fact that the Creator has obscured Himself. The Light, that is, has created distance between itself and us. We seem to exist in darkness, as if our eyes were closed. By eating the fruit, the serpent suggests, Adam and Eve's "eyes will be opened." They will reconnect with the Light. In fact, they will become the Light, "like divine beings."

Is this not, after all, what the Creator wants us to do? So it seemed to Adam and Eve, and the serpent reassures them that the connection they are about to create with the Light will be an act of sharing in God's intention. And it was, at least at first. But here Kabbalah takes the biblical narrative in a radical new direction. Because Adam and Eve were not fully constituted to receive the Light—because the Vessel had not yet *earned* an unmediated connection—they were overwhelmed by the moment in the same way that a weak electrical circuit will flash brightly and then burn out at the sudden infusion of a powerful current. The kabbalists literalize this principle through a startling addition to the narrative: *Adam and Eve took a second bite!* In the interval, a fundamental transformation had taken place, but not the positive one that had been envisioned. Rather, their desire had lost its sharing intention and had become self-serving. They were farther than ever from unity with the nature of God, and this is exactly what the serpent had intended. It is essential to understand, however, that this impasse is also an opportunity. By traversing it, we can truly prepare the Vessel. We can earn the Light. We can receive it and take fulfillment in it. Most important, we can share it.

Desire itself came into being for the sole purpose of drawing down the endless Light of the Creator, whose essence is the sharing of itself. In our world, desire is all too often for ourselves alone, without any thought of sharing. When the desire to receive for the self alone dominates consciousness without any restraint, a disconnection occurs. Through selfish acts and thoughts, we become isolated from the Creator and from the source of spiritual nourishment. Only the ephemeral pleasures remain, without the everlasting joy of the Light. As we read in the Talmud, "He who desires money will not be satisfied with money."

Nor were Adam and Eve satisfied by the fruit of the Tree of Knowledge. This is Kabbalah's interpretation of what might be called the basics of the Genesis narrative. But as the preceding Zohar passages indicate, this is only the starting point. We have spoken of Adam and Eve as a couple, but until the second bite of the fruit they were not separate at the spiritual level. This detachment took place at the same instant that the divide widened between the Vessel and the Light. Where there had been unity and equilibrium, there was now dissimilarity and fragmentation. Where there had been eternal existence in Paradise, there was now mortal life in the physical world.

This last change requires some explanation. Immortality before the fall was not just "living forever." It was immortality *consciousness*— freedom from what the Zohar calls the "evil inclination" that brings not only death to humanity, but also all other forms of pain and suffering.

After the Fall, immortality consciousness was gone, replaced by a consciousness—a knowledge—of death and evil that instantly expressed itself in the physical dimension of life. But despite all this, the plain fact of immortality remained untouched, in the same way that the signal that carries a television program remains in the air even after the set has been turned off. With the Fall of Adam, the bad news is that we stopped receiving the program. But we also began the process of repairing the receiving mechanism and getting it tuned in again. This correction, this *tikkun*, is our task for however many years it requires and however many lifetimes. When an individual human being truly completes this process, immortality is restored—as consciousness, surely, and on the level of the physical body as well. It is worth repeating that as all humanity makes collective progress toward this objective, a "critical mass" of corrected souls will eventually be achieved. This will again tip the balance toward the immortality that existed before the Fall, and we will reconnect with that reality.

But this time, when we enter Paradise, there will be an important difference: We will have earned it. We will have chosen it of our own free will. We will have overcome the obstacles that we ourselves brought into being at the time of the Fall, and through that struggle we will have made ourselves worthy.

It is an inspiring picture, but for the moment we should address a very straightforward question: Is Kabbalah declaring that someone, or perhaps anyone, can literally escape death owing to a transformation of his or her soul? The short answer is yes—but very few people achieve this level of transformation. Immortality consciousness involves much more than just changing the way we think and feel about death. In fact, it is unlikely that the great souls who achieved immortality consciousness gave much thought to death at all. But even if we do not achieve the level of spiritual elevation attained by Moses or Rabbi Shimon bar Yochai, immortality is a presence in our lives in the sense that the Zohar discusses. Even as death became part of human experience when Adam and Eve were expelled from the Garden, the process of conquering death also became a reality. Ultimately, the kabbalists explain, it is inevitable that this conquest will be realized, including our bodies' physical survival. Even now death is being conquered on the cellular level. Science and Kabbalah are in accord regarding the immortality of DNA, and in many respects their teachings are strikingly similar. For example, Rav Yehuda Ashlag taught that our reproductive power of the human species as a whole represents the expression of primordial immortality in the physical world.

Rabbi Ashlag wrote, "No man lives for himself but only for the chain as a whole. No part of the chain actually receives the Light of life (immortality) into itself, but it only transmits this Light of life to the whole chain." This is perfectly congruent with an influential theory of genetic biology, articulated for general readers by Richard Dawkins in his book *The Selfish Gene*. Dawkins describes life as a kind of perpetual motion machine, designed at the cellular level to persist forever. Paying the mortgage, having a good dinner, waiting for a particular telephone call—such things may seem important to us in our daily experience, but what *is* really important at the most fundamental level is the passing on of genetic material to a succeeding generation, and then another and another. In this way, immortality is achieved on the scale of the gene, which to nature is the only scale that really matters. We may think that our genes are attributes of our individual human identities, but according to Dawkins it is we who are appendages of our genes. We are simply vehicles for transporting them as far as possible into the future, which is where life desperately wants them to go.

And why does life want them to go there? While science chooses not to discuss the overriding direction or purpose of immortality, Kabbalah teaches that this is exactly what makes life meaningful and intelligible. Each of us is the bearer of sparks of energy from an unimaginably ancient source. That is, we are all the inheritors of Adam's soul, which fragmented through time and space at the instant of the Fall. Our bodies, our emotions, and our thoughts are all shards of the shattered primordial Vessel, personified by Adam and Eve in the Genesis narrative. As the Zohar discusses, when Adam and Eve conceived children after the expulsion from the Garden, their offspring were born from the "side of the evil inclination." They were subject to biological death. But where science recognizes no spiritual purpose in this process, Kabbalah sees it as a continuing reprise and correction of the original Fall. Kabbalah sees not just a "happy ending," but an end to the very idea of endings, and a return to the infinite Tree-of-Life reality ordained for us by the Creator.

CHAPTER 26

FORGIVENESS

T he Creator sees us at our worst moments, yet He for-
gives us and continues to give His love. This is a central
kabbalistic teaching, and one that sets Kabbalah apart
from other, more severe traditions whose influence is felt more than
we may realize. Anyone who has studied early American literature
will not forget the sermon entitled "Sinners in the Hands of an
Angry God," composed in the seventeenth century by the Puritan
minister Jonathan Edwards. Man, according to this sermon, is like
an insect that God is holding above a blazing fire. The writhing insect is an object of disgust to God, and there is absolutely no reason
why He ought not consign it to the flames. The world would be
better off if He did so. What, then, holds Him back? This question
is never answered. It is a mystery why God does not give us what we
deserve. It almost seems perverse of God not to make an end of humanity once and for all. So far He has not done so, but there is a
strong implication that He might change His mind any minute.

Kabbalah teaches that the Creator is a very different sort of
presence. Far from being disgusted by humanity, He loves us
unconditionally—not because of what we do or fail to do, but simply because this is the nature of God. Everything, after all, is God's
creation, and since He is purely good, everything He has made is
also good at its core. To the extent that we ourselves can adopt this

perspective, we draw closer to unity with the Creator. That is, we make progress toward the ultimate goal of our existence in the world.

The Zohar derives this teaching in connection with Joseph's famous interpretation of Pharaoh's dream, from which seven years of abundance were foreseen, to be followed by seven years of famine.

Vol. 6, pp. 234–237

Rabbi Aba opened with the verse, "Counsel in the heart of man is like deep water; but a man of understanding will draw it out." (Proverbs 20:5) "Counsel in the heart of man is like deep water" refers to the Creator, who gave counsel by bringing about events by the hands of Joseph, to fulfill the decree of famine upon the world. "But a man of understanding will draw it out" refers to Joseph, who revealed the meanings of the Creator's decree through the interpretation of the dream. Come and behold: Joseph not only abstained from causing evil to his brothers, he also did kindness and truth by them. This is always the way of the righteous. Therefore God always has compassion for them in this world and the world to come.

This is followed by a poignant anecdote concerning forgiveness. As often in Kabbalah, the unassuming subject of the incident is proclaimed to be greater than the patriarchs.

Near the city of Lod, a man sat on a ledge protruding from a mountainside. He was weary from the road, so he slept. While he was sleeping, a snake was coming toward him. Then a lizard appeared and killed the snake. When the man woke, he saw the dead snake. He stood up and at that moment the ledge was torn from the mountain and fell to the valley below. Thus, he was saved. Had he risen a moment later, he would have fallen and been killed.

Rabbi Aba came to him and said: "What have you done that the Creator performed for you two miracles, saving you from the snake and from the ledge that fell, for these events did not happen without reason?"

The man said: "In all my days, I forgave and made peace with any man who did evil by me. If I could not make peace with him, I did not sleep on my bed before forgiving him and all those who grieved me. Thus, I did not harbor hatred all that day for the harm anyone did me. Moreover, from that day on, I tried to do kindness by them."

Rabbi Aba wept and said: "This man's deeds exceed those of Joseph. For those who injured Joseph were his brothers; assuredly, he should have pitied them from kinship. But this man behaved so to everyone, so he is greater than Joseph and is worthy to have the Creator perform one miracle after the other for his sake."

Perhaps more than the man's forgiveness, what is really esteemed here is the refusal to assign blame. This is one of the most eloquent sections of the Zohar, and a true human expression of what Kabbalah describes as the nature of God.

He continued with the verse, "He that walks uprightly walks surely: but he that perverts his ways shall be found out." (Proverbs 10:9) "He that walks uprightly" refers to the man who walks the ways of the Torah. He will "walk surely" for no fiend in the world will be able to harm him. ". . . but he that perverts his ways shall be found out." Who shall be found out? He who deviates from the way of truth and plans to repay his evil for evil, thereby transgressing the verse, "You shall not avenge nor bear any grudge." (Leviticus 19:18)

Come and behold: He who walks the way of truth is hidden by the Creator, so that he will not be found nor recognized by the negative side, "but he that perverts his ways shall be found out" and will be known to them. Happy are the men who walk the way of truth, walk surely in the world, and have no fear in this world or the world to come.

In these few paragraphs, the Zohar is at its most prescient and is uncannily contemporary—to preach forgiveness in a world in which vengeance and warfare were considered sensible ways of organizing one's life. At the time this great book was written, it was the rule that unless a wrong was avenged there could be no peace. In stark contrast to its time, the Zohar proclaimed that unless the wrong is *forgiven* there can be no peace.

CHAPTER 27

CONNECTING TO
THE SOURCE OF LIFE

D avid is both the most puzzling and the most accessible
of the patriarchs. The arc of his life includes so many
seemingly contradictory roles. He is a gentle shepherd
and a war hero, a musician, a poet, a father, and an adulterer. The
prophet Nathan came close to calling him a murderer, yet death
also stalked David himself every day of his life.

In the Garden of Eden, the Creator granted Adam a glimpse
into the future of humanity. Every soul that would ever live, or even
have the potential to live, passed under Adam's gaze. When an unusually beautiful soul came into view, Adam was heartbroken to
discover that it would never enter the world but was destined to die
at the moment of birth. Adam then asked God if he might take
seventy years from his own life and give them to the ill-fated soul.
The request was granted, and this is how David came to walk the
earth.

But David's consciousness was never really at peace. He was
always aware that in a literal sense he was living on borrowed
time. Yet who has not had similar intimations of mortality? Perhaps it is for this reason that David, who lived so close to death,
represents the physical world in kabbalistic writings. Like the world
itself, he was strong and prodigious but also fragile.

Vol. 6, pp. 291–298

Rabbi Yehuda and Rabbi Yosi met in the village of Chanan. While they were sitting at the inn, a traveler came with a baggage-laden mule and entered the house. Rabbi Yehuda was then saying to Rabbi Yosi: "It is said that King David slept like a horse. If this is true, how did he wake up at midnight? The portion of sixty breaths of a horse's sleep is very brief, so he would have awakened before even a third of the night was over."

Rabbi Yosi replied: "When night fell, King David used to sit with the princes of his house to execute justice and study the Torah. He did not go to sleep when night fell, but not until much later. He then slept until midnight, when he woke and rose to worship the Creator with songs and hymns."

During sleep, the Zohar explains, fifty-nine of sixty parts of our soul leave the body; only one-sixtieth remains to sustain us physically. When the body is in slumber, the chains of physical existence are actually broken. The soul is free to ascend to a high place in the spiritual atmosphere, where it can connect to the sharing energy of the Light unencumbered by the physical body's inherent desire to receive for itself alone.

The traveler interposed and asked: Is this what you think? Here is the secret of the matter: King David is alive and exists forever. He was careful to avoid a foretaste of death—and because sleep is a sixtieth part of death, King David, whose domain is that of the living, slept only sixty breaths. For up to sixty breaths less one, it is living; from then on, a man tastes death, and the side of the impure spirit reigns over him.

King David guarded himself from tasting death, lest the side of the impure spirit obtain control over him. For sixty breaths minus one are the Secret of Supernal Life.

This last sentence deserves attention. Why not sixty breaths minus two, or even sixty breaths minus fifty-nine, in order to really play it safe? Kabbalah teaches that to have a connection with the Upper Worlds, we must challenge ourselves to the limit here below. David, as we saw in chapter 22, asked the Creator to test him, because he knew that an untested soul could never join the ranks of the patriarchs. Aware of his vulnerability, he chose to live life to the limit in order to fulfill a high spiritual purpose.

Therefore King David would measure the hours until midnight, so as to remain alive, lest the foretaste of death dominate him. At midnight, David would be in his domain, waking up and uttering chants and hymns. For when midnight stirred, David did not wish to be found connected to another domain, the domain of death.

Midnight is the best time for study and prayer. While most people sleep, the spiritual atmosphere is unusually clear. Just as night radio, with fewer channels competing for the airwaves, often can be tuned in with greater clarity, prayer and study at this hour are less encumbered by the static and chaos of the masses of humanity.

When midnight comes Supernal Holiness is awakened, but if a man is asleep and does not awaken to regard the glory of his Master, he becomes attached to the other side. King David therefore always woke at midnight, careful of the glory of his Master, alive before the Living One, and he would never sleep long enough to taste death. Thus, he slept the sixty breaths of a horse—sixty breaths less one.

Rabbi Yehuda and Rabbi Yosi kissed the traveler, for he had revealed a new explanation concerning midnight prayer. They asked him: "What is your name?" He replied: "Chizkiyah" (lit. "strengthened of Hashem"). They said to him: "May you be strengthened and may your study of the Torah be augmented." Rabbi Yehuda said: "Since you have already begun, tell us more of the Supernal Mysteries to which you have made reference."

While they were talking, Rabbi Elazar came. When he saw them he said: "Assuredly the Shechinah is here. What are you discussing?" When they told him what the traveler had said, Rabbi Elazar replied: "He spoke well. The six hours before midnight pertain to life, both in the Upper World and in this one. After midnight, there are sixty other breaths, which are all on the side of death, and the grade of death is upon them."

King David cleaved to the sixty breaths of life. But afterward, he slept not at all. This is the meaning of, "I will not give sleep to my eyes, nor slumber to my eyelids." (Psalms 132:4) Thus the traveler spoke well, for David should be considered alive. He is on the side of the living and not on the side of death.

Come and behold: Whoever sings the praises of the Torah during the night before God is strengthened by day. For a thread of grace emerges from the right side and is drawn upon him, and he is strengthened by it. David therefore said: "Lord of my salvation, when I cry in the night before you." He continued: " 'The dead cannot praise the Creator' (Psalms 115:17), because it is the living who should praise the Living, and not the dead." Then Chizkiyah said: " 'The living shall praise you, as I do' (Isaiah 38:19), for the living have a connection with the Living. So is King David living, and he is near the One who lives forever. And whoever approaches the One living is living, as it is written: 'But you that did cleave to the Creator are alive every one of you this day.' " (Deuteronomy 4:4)

We must connect to the source of life in order to remain alive. This is what is meant by "the living have a connection with the living." This is an act of will, particularly as we get older, when the desire for an end can assert itself as selfishly as any other bodily need. Until we gain access to the teachings of Kabbalah, it may seem that we are born into this mysterious universe with no apparent set of instructions, no maps or equations, no signs or guideposts, nothing but our own equally unfathomable instincts, intuitions, and reasoning abilities to tell us where we came from, why we are here, and what we are supposed to do. The Zohar itself is the guide that we seek. What we do possess—and this is the key to our spiritual transformation—is a passionate need to live, a fervent wish for the story to go on. But we ourselves must keep turning the pages.

IN CONCLUSION

Kabbalah is a practical guide for transforming chaos and fragmentation into unity and completion. Since the time of Adam chaos has held sway in the physical world. Slowly but surely, however, through the work of the righteous and the spiritual growth of humanity as a whole, we have moved ever closer to transformation, fulfillment, and ultimate oneness with God. As this journey continues, the Zohar is our most precious guide and our most valuable tool. Let me be very clear as to why this is the case.

Chaos currently afflicts humanity in two basic forms. First, the transcendent, spiritual side of our nature is largely disconnected from our consciousness as a whole. The subconscious mind asserts itself largely through neurosis, depression, and other forms of psychopathology, while the sparks of the Divine that exist in all of us remain hidden. We therefore live each day without access to our own unlimited potential. The rational, empirical, scientific powers of the human mind have wrought such seeming miracles that there seems no point in looking for the wonders that lie elsewhere in our makeup, though in fact they are infinitely greater. Kabbalah teaches that, if we are to avail ourselves of our full potential, a bridge of some sort is needed between everyday consciousness and our inner transformative powers. The Zohar provides this bridge. Through its narratives of surprise happenings, sudden insights, and full-blown epiphanies, the Zohar subverts conventional expectations of what life really entails. A walk through the countryside or a visit to an inn can turn into a startling revelation of truth. Further, since physical settings are always emblematic of spiritual conditions in kabbalistic writings, the Zohar shows how even the mental equivalent of a leisurely stroll can and should lead to insight and transformation.

If the Zohar serves to connect us to a concealed part of ourselves, however, it also empowers us to *disconnect* from the pervasive static of the modern world—the negative energy that blocks our ability to achieve fulfillment and completion in our innermost hearts, and to find clear direction in our everyday lives. How does the Zohar accomplish this? It is not by dint of hard intellectual work or strenuous mental exercise. This could hardly be the case, for even scanning the Hebrew letters of the Zohar has profound benefits. Simply putting ourselves in the presence of the text literally works wonders. Some might compare this effect to the use of mantras in Eastern spiritual traditions, in which patterns of sound that have no referent in the physical world foster clarity and detachment from ongoing inner dialog. The mantralike aspects of the Zohar are worth considering, but Kabbalah describes the book's effects in terms less psychological and more connected to the physical sciences. The Zohar is literally a kind of lightning rod. It draws the Light of the Creator to us and reveals the Light in ourselves. In so doing, it eliminates inner darkness, for darkness cannot coexist with Light. Nor can chaos, whose essence is disconnection, remain in force when a genuine connection with the Upper World has taken place.

The Zohar revolutionizes our consciousness, enhancing both the quality of our daily lives and the evolution of our souls. For the kabbalist, the Zohar is nothing less than a time machine and a teleportation device all in one; by replacing doubt with certainty and darkness with Light, it erases the limits that the physical world places on us. With it, we see where we are, where we have been, and where we are going—the future, the past, and the present, all as one.

With the Zohar and all of Kabbalah becoming more accessible to people throughout the world, we are witness to the start of a new age of revelation.

Today, more than at any other time in history, the Light demands to be revealed, as it is written in the Talmud, "More than the calf wants to suckle, the cow wants to be milked." Until now, the spiritual development of humanity has been left to humanity itself, and this endeavor has failed to bring real joy and fulfillment to the world, notwithstanding the material abundance that surrounds us. Over six millennia, the human mind has brought forth many practical innovations and even some genuine spiritual revelations, but so far that has not eradicated the ills of the world. But as the twenty-first century begins, a new level of consciousness has come into being. We can attribute this to the Light of God itself, which heretofore has existed at a certain remove from humanity's journey toward a higher awareness. But the Creator has observed the overwhelming obstacles that have appeared during the course of that journey, and as has happened from time to time in the biblical narrative, He has chosen to intervene. The Light will now begin to fulfill His desire to share His full beneficence. And the Zohar, including this relatively brief selection, is the instrument of that fulfillment. I am confident that this book will lead a great many people to explore the full text of this sacred work, and that their lives will be immeasurably enriched as a result.

May God bless us all.

BIBLIOGRAPHY AND SOURCES FOR FURTHER READING

The Zohar: The First Ever Unabridged English Translation, with Commentary (Rabbi Michael Berg, ed., 22 vols.). New York and Los Angeles: The Kabbalah Centre, 2001.

Sefer Yetzirah: The Book of Creation in Theory and Practice (Aryeh Kaplan, ed.). York Beach, Maine: Samuel Weiser, Inc., 1997.

Ashlag, Rabbi Yehuda. *An Entrance to the Zohar* (Dr. Philip S. Berg, ed.). New York and Jerusalem: The Research Centre of Kabbalah, 1974.

———. *A Gift of the Bible*. New York and Jerusalem: The Research Centre of Kabbalah, 1984.

———. *Ten Luminous Emanations* (compiled and edited by Rav P. S. Berg, 2 vols.). New York and Jerusalem: The Research Centre of Kabbalah, 1973.

Berg, Rav P. S. *Education of a Kabbalist*. New York and Los Angeles: The Kabbalah Centre, 2000.

———. *Immortality: The Rise and Fall of the Angel of Death*. New York, Los Angeles, Tel Aviv: The Kabbalah Centre, 1999.

———. *Kabbalistic Astrology*. New York, Los Angeles, Tel Aviv: The Kabbalah Centre, 2000.

———. *Secret Codes of the Universe*. New York, Los Angeles, Tel Aviv: The Kabbalah Centre, 2000.

———. *Wheels of a Soul* (revised edition). New York, Los Angeles, Jerusalem: The Kabbalah Centre, 1995.

Berg, Michael. *The Way: Using the Wisdom of Kabbalah for Spiritual Transformation and Fulfillment.* New York: John Wiley & Sons, 2001.

Kaplan, Aryeh. *The Bahir.* York Beach, Maine: Samuel Weiser, Inc., 1989.

Luzzatto, Rabbi Moshe Chaim. *The Path of the Just.* Jerusalem and New York: Feldheim Publishers, 1966.

———. *The Way of God.* Jerusalem and New York: Feldheim Publishers, 1996.

INDEX

Aaron (biblical figure), 191, 205, 207–10

Aba, Rabbi, 43–47, 50–55, 117, 219, 245, 253, 254

Abraham (biblical figure), 49, 87, 126, 130, 222

  appearance of Shechinah, 70–73

  binding of Isaac, 146–52

  circumcision, 67–69, 79

  genealogies, 60

  God's tests, 61, 62, 217

  greatness, 61, 64, 144

  as historical figure, 66

  journey from own country, 50, 59–60, 88–89

  kindness and mercy, 42, 63

  refusal of idol worship, 62

  and Sarah, 73–74

Achievement, 122

Achilles, 219

Adam (biblical figure), 98, 103, 125, 126, 159, 211, 212, 214

  and David, 256

  Fall of, 85, 249, 251

  in Garden of Eden, 136, 166, 245

  Jacob as reincarnation of, 156, 158

  and Klipah, 82–83

  nakedness, 101

  progeny, 244–45, 251

  repentance, 113–21

  second bite, 248–49

  and serpent, 160, 247

  temptation by grapes, 99, 139

Addiction, 86

Aeneid (Virgil), 223

Afflictions, 178, 179–80, 184, 187

Afterlife, 133–34

Agriculture, 126

Akiva ben Joseph, Rabbi, 7, 8, 91, 121

Alexander the Great, 219

Alkabetz, Shlomo, 6

Angel of Darkness, 99, 100, 130, 137, 139–41, 143–45, 165

Angels, 83, 123, 126

Anonymity, 46, 50

Anthropic principle, 238

ABOUT THE AUTHOR

Kabbalist Rav P. S. Berg was born in the Williamsburg section of Brooklyn, New York. Ordained at Torah VaDaat in Williamsburg in 1951, Rav Berg studied in Israel under Rav Yehuda Brandwein, from whom he inherited the leadership of The Kabbalah Centre in 1969. A kabbalistic master who comes from a long lineage of masters, Rav Berg has dedicated his life to making what had been a secret and obscure wisdom available to all people, while diligently preserving the authenticity of its message. The Rav is dean and codirector of The Kabbalah Centre, the leading educational organization devoted to teaching Kabbalah. He lectures and teaches internationally and meets with spiritual and world leaders for the purpose of fostering global peace and spiritual understanding.

The Rav has touched the lives of millions through his many books, including *Immortality, Wheels of a Soul, To the Power of One, Miracles, Mysteries, and Prayer, Secret Codes of the Universe* and *Education of a Kabbalist.* Under his guidance, The Kabbalah Centre has published the first complete English translation of and commentary on the Zohar, which is now available in twenty-two volumes.